The Ultimate Insi... To Winning Found...

A Foundation CEO Reveals the Secrets
You Need to Know

First printed May 2012

10 9 8 7 6 5 4 3 2

Printed in the United States of America

This text is printed on acid-free paper.

Emerson & Church, Publishers
15 Brook Street, Medfield, MA 02052
Tel. 508-359-0019
Fax 508-359-2703
www.emersonandchurch.com

Library of Congress Cataloging-in-Publication Data

Teitel, Martin.
  The ultimate insider's guide to winning foundation grants : a
foundation CEO reveals the secrets you need to know / Martin
Teitel ; foreword by Amy Goldman. — Expanded 2nd ed.
      p. cm.
  Rev. ed. of: Thank you for submitting your proposal. c2006.
  ISBN 978-1-889102-16-0 (pbk. : alk. paper) 1. Proposal
writing for grants. 2. Fund raising. I. Teitel, Martin. Thank you
for submitting your proposal. II. Title.
  HG177.T45 2012
  658.15'224—dc23
                              2011047776

The Ultimate Insider's Guide To Winning Foundation Grants

**A Foundation CEO Reveals The Secrets
You Need to Know**

MARTIN TEITEL

Foreword by Amy Goldman

A Revised and Expanded Edition of
"Thank You for Submitting Your Proposal"

Emerson
& Church
PUBLISHERS

FOREWORD

Marty Teitel is the ultimate insider and the book you're holding is the ultimate guide to winning foundation grants.

As a funder and board member of both national and community-oriented nonprofits, I've known Marty for over 20 years. He's a highly principled and effective leader – a person to emulate. Perhaps what I most admire is his unassailable integrity. Marty's a fierce defender of what's right and good, a joyous person who sees the best in others but is never fooled by deception and dishonesty.

This book contains the best insights and advice any grant-seeker is likely to find. In many ways, it's a style manual for fundraisers, containing everything you need to know about the process of applying for foundation grants.

Marty debunks myths about charitable foundations and gives the inside scoop. You'll find plenty of commonsense counsel on what to do and pitfalls to avoid. Helpful hints are embedded within colorful accounts and war stories, some of which will make you cringe.

The meat of the book is how to write funding requests, including short letters of inquiry and full-blown proposals. Here Marty has *really* nailed it. Funders look for prospective grantees who can express themselves clearly and succinctly in written language. Marty and I know from experience that people who write successful proposals are better planners and more likely to get things done in the world.

Marty's book is immensely practical and filled with sage advice. If you want foundation funding to achieve your aims, and do good for others, then you've come to the right place. Knowing how funders think, what they value in potential grantees, and how they operate can help demystify the process, promote understanding, and significantly increase your chances of winning a grant.

Marty has helped disperse tens of millions of dollars to worthy recipients during his long and distinguished career as a foundation staffer. But before that, he was a nonprofit leader, strapped for cash, begging and borrowing resources. As a result, he has a deep understanding of the mindset, virtues, and faults of players on both sides of the equation. Marty advocates enforceable standards of practice for grant-makers. And he makes excellent suggestions for everyone on how to increase civility, common courtesy, and mutual respect.

The *Ultimate Insider's Guide to Winning Foundation Grants* is the distilled wisdom of a remarkable man and is written in a lively, conversational way. Marty has a wicked sense of humor and a sharp wit. He comes through on the page as the man I've always known in the field: good-hearted, down-to-earth, solid. I trust his voice, and I trust him.

Amy Goldman   *Lillian Goldman Charitable Trust*

CONTENTS

INTRODUCTION

Thirty-five years ago, running a tiny nonprofit in San Francisco, I was on the phone with the electric company, trying to convince them to let us go another two weeks without paying our bill, until a hoped-for check came in. I couldn't help it – as I pleaded with them my voice cracked, as if I were going to cry. We were given the extension.

When I looked up from the call, the other staff – all of whom were behind in being paid – quickly looked down at their work in embarrassment. I collected myself and announced, "In my next life, I'm going to be a funder."

Within a year, my prayers were answered, and I began the first of a number of jobs working for people who give money away, instead of those who constantly seek it.

In my long career as a funder, I loved the satisfaction of helping people who were doing wonderful things for other people, not to mention the regular paychecks. But I've never forgotten that San Francisco job, or others I've held in the hardscrabble world of grant-seeking nonprofits.

In this book, I want to share, as openly and frankly as I can, what I learned during my time as a funder. My hope is to provide tools that will help you increase your chances of winning the support you need.

In the years since that awful day in San Francisco, I've met with an army of grant seekers, I've read many thousands of proposals, and I've had a hand in dispensing many millions of dollars. Along the way I've learned a few things about what works – and what doesn't.

During that time, I actually saw few proposals that advocated for bad ideas. But I encountered an astonishing number of funding requests that were cast in the worst possible light, and even more that were clearly directed to the wrong funding source. For years I've thought about how much everyone, grant seekers and grant makers alike, could benefit from some candid information.

When I sat down with my staff each week to review the latest crop of funding requests, what were we looking for? How did we really make our screening decisions? What was it like on the inside?

Although I surely can't speak for all funders, I can share some of how the grant-making process actually works. By doing so, I hope to help grant seekers as well as those of us who give money away, by increasing the chances that worthy funding requests end up in the right hands.

Recently I retired from forty-four years in the nonprofit world, most of those years granting money. Without a foundation paycheck, I'm free to tell it like it is. Thus, this book – a handbook that's divided into four sections.

The first, Thank You for Your Proposal, has detailed chapters on each element of the grant-seeking process, distilled from the many thousands of proposals and scores of foundation board meetings I've been exposed to over my career.

Sometimes the conventional wisdom leads us astray. Part Two, Myths about Foundations, explores some of the misinformation that has a stubborn hold on some in the grant-seeker world – to the detriment of us all.

Part Three, The Grant Seeker's Reality Check, is organized as a how-to guide for those of you who work in the grant-seeker trenches as well as board members and others who want to get a handle on how the process really works, from the perspective of those who make the grants.

Part Four, Administering the Truth-Detector Test to America's Charitable Foundations, presents detailed answers to actual questions I was asked over the years. It's likely you'll find some of your questions there as well.

Here's wishing you the best of luck with your proposal.

CHAPTER 1

Not-So Divided Loyalties: Whom Does the Funder Work For?

Our country finances itself by adopting a budget and then compelling its citizens to pay taxes to support what the government spends. When someone doesn't pay taxes, the rest of us have to pay a little more to compensate.

The 76,000 private foundations in our country pay little in taxes – usually 1 or 2 percent of what they earn. And donors to foundations can deduct from their own tax bills the thousands or millions they contribute.

In exchange for this rather sweet deal with the government, foundations are required to spend their money on "educational, scientific, and charitable" purposes. In other words, they have to do something for the public good.

If you think the amounts involved are pocket change, you're mistaken. U.S. foundations have assets well in excess of half a trillion dollars, distributing more than $35 billion in grants annually.

Given that all of us who pay taxes undeniably pay more because of the billions of foundation dollars that aren't fully taxed or taxed at all, we all (literally) have an interest in what foundations do. Even, perhaps, in how they treat people – themselves taxpayers – who ask for money.

A few years ago, when I was raising money for an organization, I called a foundation officer in New York whom I knew from our mutual service on a committee. I told her I had a good idea for a project that fit the work she was doing. She asked me to put it on one page and call her back in two weeks.

Those of you who are experienced fundraisers may know what's coming next. I called the program officer back fourteen days later and asked what she thought of my letter. "What letter?" she barked. I persisted as inoffensively as I could, finally inducing her to look on her desk, where she found the unread letter. I told her how I wouldn't mind in the slightest if she read the letter while I waited quietly on the phone (it had taken me two days to get through, and I didn't want to hang up and start all over).

There was a long silence. Then she blurted out, "This is stupid!" "Oh," I said brightly, as if she'd just offered to buy me lunch, "What might I have left out?" "Well," she said, "you don't mention a single person I know. You can't possibly know what you're doing. Bye." Click.

Not all foundation people are that unswervingly impolite. But those of you who have approached some of the nation's 76,000 foundations know that there are nearly as many sets of guidelines and rules as there are funders – and a huge variation in how people are treated, ranging from well mannered to creatively egregious.

Why worry about behavior and tax and accountability issues? What you really want to know is "How do I get the money?" The conundrum of funder accountability matters for two reasons. First, *you have a right* to ask for money: in a real sense, it is your money! And approaching the task of grant seeking can and should be based on holding your head high, not groveling for largess, but requesting a share of what is yours.

Second, the story about the one-page letter illustrates the other startling fact of foundation fundraising. Your morale and even sanity will be improved if you don't expect fairness, justice, or rationality – not to mention basic courtesy. Fundraising is like what dating in high school was for many of us: hard work intertwined with great risk and continual rejection. It will go better if you can find a way not to take it personally.

■ Who's in Charge Here?

During my decades of funding, I occasionally called on my colleagues as I traveled around visiting grantees and attending meetings. I got to see some pretty spiffy digs: cascading fountains in the lobbies, exquisite art, ergonomic conference room chairs, and the very latest in computer technology.

To be sure, some funding administrators work in modest

surroundings. And, according to the Council on Foundation's annual compensation surveys, a number of them make less than those employed at the agencies they fund. But on the whole, working for a foundation is pretty nice: good pay, excellent fringe benefits, pleasant surroundings, sometimes even first-class travel. It's easy to see how some people can begin to confuse their imposing surroundings with personal weightiness.

Aside from perks, perhaps the greatest jeopardy to individual modesty in the funding business is something I touched on earlier: funders have lots of scarcely accountable power. Having power doesn't mean it's abused, but having it does mean a person can come to feel he or she deserves it.

Back when I ran a foundation in California, we had a huge flow of proposals, so many that we had to use big metal carts to wheel the weekly load up and down the hallway. We even added on a storage building for all of the file cabinets of paperwork. Out of all those thousands of proposals, we rejected 95 percent!

The quick and simple act of coding a proposal for rejection meant that some hard-working group might not make payroll, or that a genuinely beneficial and worthy piece of work might never happen.

Making those heavy decisions all day can gradually convince a program officer that *her* judgment is what really matters, that *she* is the one who's actually shaping what happens out in the world, not those pesky grantees.

This misconception leads to a well-known occupational

hazard among funders: high-and-mightiness. Arrogance. Self-absorption. Few of us in the funding business attribute these qualities to ourselves, but almost every one of us can privately point to others who exemplify the famous egotism of the profession. I'm fine, but you ought to see *that other guy.*

The truth is far from what you see in the haughty demeanor and posh surroundings in many foundation offices. The reality is that many funders are far less powerful than we (or they) might believe.

In a few foundations, mostly clustered at the top of the asset range, program officers and executive directors actually do have real power to decide what the money is spent on. But in most foundations, actual power lies elsewhere, and funder strutting is mainly puffery.

This distinction is important because grant seekers focus a great deal of attention on foundation staff – are they barking up the wrong tree?

According to federal and most state laws, the responsibility for deciding where a foundation puts its money rests with the board of directors. The board has other responsibilities too, such as making sure funds are invested prudently and that various federal and state rules are followed. Board members, and in some instances top staff, bear *personal* liability for the acts and omissions of the foundation.

I should know. I was held liable years ago when a foundation I headed briefly employed an inept bookkeeper who missed a federal payroll tax payment.

By the time the government figured it out, the interest and fines had increased to almost ten times the missed payment. Because I was the legal "foundation manager," the IRS held me personally responsible, even though the bookkeeper was long gone and I had no idea she'd forgotten the tax. I had to pay the missed taxes and penalties out of my own pocket, and the foundation was prohibited from reimbursing me.

From this story there are two lessons we can learn about how foundations work. For one thing, foundation boards and top managers are forever being "admonished" by their lawyers and accountants.

We pay people in expensive suits to come to our offices periodically and scare us into acting in a prudent way. And to the extent that bathing funders in this continuing stream of cautions makes them less likely to do foolish or even corrupt things, it's good for all of us. Yet it also can make funders risk averse and obsessed with avoiding scandal.

Grant seekers who approach foundations with a less-than-straightforward accounting of what they're up to do so at great peril, as we'll see when we talk about proposals.

The other central fact of foundation boards is that, although most hire staff to serve as a barrier between them and grant seekers, it is the board, not the staff, that determines and enforces the funding guidelines.

This is the single most important fact you can know in dealing with foundation staff: *no matter how important they act, no matter how lovely and imposing their surroundings, it is likely they're functionaries carrying out the decisions of other – invisible – people.*

When I win the lottery and establish my own foundation, it'll give money only to the causes I favor. In the meantime, the foundations that employ people like me make sure – via their boards – that staff members pay attention to the causes the foundation's donor, as interpreted by the board, wants supported. Most foundation employees like those causes and are glad to help, but funder functionaries are instruments of the will of others, not independent agents.

Therefore, good foundation fundraising should begin, and in a sense end, with finding out what the board considers important. No matter how misguided their guidelines and strategies may seem, there's no point in arguing. It only annoys the people you're trying to convince to help you.

In addition to the published guidelines, foundations always give you another valuable look into what they consider important: the grants list. This is where they've put their money; there is no more certain indicator of what a foundation actually cares about. Most foundations list their grants on their Web sites, or they may publish grants lists, which they'll send you. If you must, get the foundation's IRS Form 990-PF.

CHAPTER 2

Let the Games Begin:
Letters of Inquiry

One day, quite a few years ago, I went to see a colleague in a behemoth foundation on the West Coast. I sat in the waiting room (yes, funders keep other funders waiting, too), watching the receptionist work. In between answering the phone and greeting me, she snapped her gum and sorted through a stack of flat manila envelopes – obviously proposals.

The young woman would glance at the return address and the cover letter, and then enter information into her computer. Just about every foundation I know has some version of this process, logging in proposals so they can be tracked. The classic foundation form letters ("... while many proposals describe interesting and important work, we regret that limited funds ...") are emitted from these databases of supplicants.

After logging in the proposal, the receptionist read a bit more on the first page, and with a few of the packets flipped back a page or two. Then, and my jaw still drops at the thought, *she tossed various proposals into the wastebasket next to her desk.* She'd put every fifth or tenth one into a folder and place it on top of a depressingly small stack on her desk.

I don't know who this individual was or her qualifications; maybe she was the world's youngest PhD in astrophysics and was simply covering the receptionist's desk briefly. It doesn't matter. What I saw was what could have been days and weeks of work -- an entire organization's hopes and plans and dreams – receiving fewer than sixty seconds of cursory screening (if *screening* is the word). And I have some reason to believe that, although this particular foundation's screening technique seems a bit pitiless even in a normally hard-edged business, it is far from unique.

I won't defend any funder who disrespectfully gives short shrift to the hard work of the world's proposal writers, but those of us on the receiving end *can* point with exasperation to the enormous volume of junk proposals that wend our way.

People find or buy lists of funders, plug them into their databases, and send out what must be immense numbers of generic proposals. Maybe once in a while this scattershot technique works. I suppose if you went to a mall looking for a ham sandwich, started at one end and went to every single store with your request, you might eventually stumble into a place that could fix you up – after having wasted the time of the puzzled clerks in the Apple Store and Talbot's.

Although no one keeps statistics about the internal workings of foundations, anecdotally it seems certain that more and more foundations are shunning unsolicited proposals. Instead, some foundations, especially those making very large grants or hard science awards, send out RFPs: requests for proposals. The RFPs describe in some detail what will be funded and how to apply.

But for most foundations the standard technique is to require LOIs instead of RFPs (foundations rival the military in their love of acronyms).

LOIs – letters of inquiry – are an example of a genuine win-win situation. Foundations avoid an avalanche of paper, and grantees are spared writing and sending thick stacks of verbiage, charts, and testimonials.

A letter of inquiry distills the organization's request down to something quite brief. It gives the foundation an opportunity to express interest, and if the putative grantee has his ears open, a chance for him to learn what tweaking of the idea might actually result in a grant.

Before we look at the LOI itself, let's look at how one foundation – one I used to run – handles letters of inquiry. As part of an entirely quirky industry, foundations are quite free to invent whatever system suits their purposes. So what I'm describing here is just an example.

The person whose job included opening the mail every day pulled out what appeared to her to be LOIs. You're about to encounter the only sports metaphor you'll read in this entire book, for which I apologize. My rule for many years was "The tie goes to the runner." How I understood this rule was that if we weren't sure something was actually a letter of inquiry, we treated it like one. A bit later we'll return to this point, since you might be surprised to learn how difficult it is for us dense funders to read the minds of grant seekers.

At any rate, the person opening the mail recorded the basic information of the LOI in a simple database and then mailed a pre-printed postcard that essentially said, "We received your letter of inquiry. If we want to know anything more about it we will contact you, otherwise you won't hear from us again."

Lest you think sending this acknowledgement is a rare instance of funder courtesy, be assured that, although many of us are fans of good manners, the card's main purpose was to reduce the volume of calls asking, "Did you get what I sent you?" For a massive organization, the U.S. Postal Service is highly efficient, and I'm not aware that any of those calls told us of something we didn't already know. But the impulse to telephone and make sure the LOI arrived is entirely understandable. Thus our postcard.

Now enshrined in a folder, the letter of inquiry was passed to a program officer for review. A very bright and well-qualified young man, in the case of our office, had this particular task in his job description because, to be honest, he had the least seniority. The fact that foundation staff members don't like to process LOIs may be useful information for you to know, and we're going to return to this point when we construct the road map to a successful letter of inquiry.

The program officer then read the LOI. Yes, he really did. As he read, he pulled up a pre-made Excel spreadsheet and pecked at it, filling in basic information such as the topic of the proposal, the essential strategy being used, and a *one-sentence* summary of the letter of inquiry. Did you get that? Your complex and subtle organization's life, already stripped of nuance by being reduced to a three-page LOI, was now further condensed to a box on a spreadsheet.

When a week or two had gone by, the program officer e-mailed the spreadsheet to his boss, the deputy director, and the foundation's executive director. (In a larger foundation more people might be in the loop, but not necessarily, say my colleagues, since foundations with bigger bucks are often organized into departments – mine was not.)

The young man's covering e-mail respectfully cajoled the recipients to read the spreadsheet before arriving at the LOI meeting. Although many in philanthropy are fans of letters of inquiry, they don't always like the process of going through them, as it's a bit like panning for gold: you have to sort through an awful lot of gravel before coming upon that little bright flash.

On the scheduled LOI morning, when I ran the foundation, we'd put our coffee mugs on the conference room table while the young man thumped down the stack of LOIs. By then I'd probably printed out my copy of the spreadsheet and scribbled a bit on it, trying my hardest not to pre-judge based on the barest of summaries.

The program officer led us through the list, in the order on the spreadsheet, which meant in the order received. He told us the name of the proposal in his hand. Often, everyone chirped, "Nope, not a fit." The program officer made a note in the "outcome" box on his spreadsheet, and we moved on. It was over in five seconds.

But occasionally one of us said, "Let me look at that." Something in the strategy box or the topic of the proposed work was interesting. If I was the one asking to see the paperwork, I'd usually glance first at the letterhead (to see if it had an advisory panel or board of directors listed). After that I'd flip right to the budget, ignoring the cover letter. Who the people involved were, and how they allocated their resources, often determined for me if it would be worth it to read the actual LOI.

At other times an idea would catch fire in our meeting, and people would start to pass the folder around and point out aspects of the proposed work that interested them. This process could result in the LOI being assigned to one of us for further investigation. My role as curmudgeon-in-chief was also to stop us from getting too fired up. I'd often say, "I agree this is a neat idea. Can anyone sitting here really picture our board voting for a grant to something this far from our guidelines?" More often than not, the nays had it.

In a typical batch of twenty letters of inquiry, it would be ordinary for two to be flagged for follow-up. But it wouldn't be remarkable for there to be none. When that happened, the staff kind of dragged out of the meeting, disappointed.

I'll tell you something about foundation staff, and I've been acquainted with quite a few. They like working on proposals, and they like making grants. Contrary to what my children will tell you, saying "no" isn't my greatest pleasure in life. I bring this up to emphasize the fact that your success in getting a grant is linked to your ability to connect constructively with someone *who is already inclined to help.*

Let's leave these funders to their room-temperature coffee and turn our focus more directly to the art and science of creating letters of inquiry.

A typical LOI will have a title, a one- or two-sentence summary of the entire project, an explanation of the issue and how it'll be addressed, and a description of the organization doing the work. A budget is always attached. Foundations vary in their requirements, but three pages plus budget make up a typical letter of inquiry. What you have here is a proposal in miniature.

What I've observed is that grantee enthusiasts, faced with the task of constructing a three-page letter of inquiry, make one of two mistakes – sometimes both. They either give themselves permission to write four or five or ten pages, because they're convinced they can capture the funder's attention, or they take their twenty-page proposal and hack away until it's three pages long – and entirely unintelligible.

What is needed instead is concise and powerful prose that evokes the content and spirit of the project in a very small space. This is not a shorter version of the full proposal but actually a different piece of writing that fulfills a distinctive function.

Let's go through the elements of a typical letter of inquiry, starting with the title of your work. Suppose you're a group of soccer parents who want to work with several local school systems. Your hope is that they'll adopt integrated pest management practices instead of spreading nasty chemicals on the fields where your kids run around after school every day.

So you could indeed send out a funding request called, "Integrating Contemporary Pest Management and Soil Amendment Regimes in Outdoor Recreation Facilities for School-Age Children and Other Young Citizens in Middlesex County." Or you could call what you are doing "The Safe Soccer League." Or "The Organic Sports Federation."

Whatever you call it, make it brief and catchy: the single purpose of naming your project is to induce the screener to read further. That's all. It's not to make the case or argue your brief. That can come later, if your LOI isn't languishing in the wastebasket.

Let's move on to the summary. Some people call this the elevator speech: how you tell someone the totality of what you're doing while riding between the fourth floor and the lobby. This task is challenging for many of us.

The summary has three standards. If you are to have

any chance of success, you must achieve all three of them:

- Concise – every word must count
- Compelling – no vacuous buzzwords
- Clear – eliminate any chance of ambiguity or misreading

Many years ago I ran an international relief program with teams of people all over the world. With no phone service and letters taking weeks to arrive, we relied on cables – international telegrams. The cables were expensive and had to be concise, often limited to under a dozen words. We spent a lot of time constructing succinct messages that left no room for mistakes in interpretation. Giving people instructions about what to do next in war zones can't leave room for doubt.

A normally loquacious person, I was challenged by this part of my job. Here are some lessons I learned in those pre-Internet days, and subsequently from many years of reading funding request summaries:

1) Your central and first step is to ask a question – sometimes a group of people can do this together: "What, in one brief sentence, are we doing?" Answering a question seems to help, and groups often come up with the right words when one person is stuck.

2) If you put 50 percent of your LOI effort into the summary, half of that effort should be directed toward writing a brilliant opening sentence. I really mean this. If you earmark four hours for writing your letter of inquiry, then you should work on the summary for two hours, an hour of which is just laboring over, and coming

back to, that first sentence.

3) Learn from, but don't emulate, professional marketers. That is, make your prose interesting, riveting if you can. But don't write something that sounds like you're selling dish soap. Like professional marketers, you need to know your audience and then create a tone best suiting your purpose. You want the foundation to "buy" your product but without seeming like your goal is selling instead of creating a partnership.

4) Avoid the sticky pit of buzzwords. Don't claim your work is "unique" or "cutting edge" or "raises awareness." Words and phrases like these are (a) unsupported general claims or (b) impossible to know or verify. And beware of flowery adjectives and vague generalities. They don't create an impression of competence, and they won't cause your LOI to stand out from the pile of pithy prose.

5) Instead, let your summary be filled with facts, concrete verbs, and sentences that show action. Emulate the writing of good journalists in mainstream newspapers: be an objective-seeming reporter who lets words create a response, rather than manipulating, exhorting, or lecturing the reader. As they teach in journalism school, "Show, don't tell."

To illustrate a few of these points, let's stay with my imaginary example from above, which comes to mind since in real life I did once live across from a soccer field. Which of these entirely fictional LOI summaries works better for you?

A) This innovative program seeks to make a unique contribution to the field of lawn care and athletic field husbandry while maintaining a health-inducing atmosphere for soccer players and providing a unique opportunity to meet our goals and objectives in addressing the scourge of chemical companies worldwide and making chemistry information available to the entire country through our model project.

B) The State Department of Health says that as many as 1,000 young people are poisoned by lawn chemicals each year. Our organization is protecting children who play on the county's athletic fields by adopting a list of 57 safe and effective methods of sports field care.

Choice A is wordy, a combination of vague and inflammatory terms, and is really beside the point. After slogging through A, the program officer may still be unclear about what's going on – provided by the end of that impossibly lengthy sentence she is still awake.

Choice B starts with a grabber (which I made up; don't pull your kid out of soccer). The second sentence then says what you're going to do – enough to paint a picture but not enough to thwart the reader's interest in learning more. The other thing about that sentence is that its claims are modest, quite positive, and there's no blame or finger-pointing.

Since I bring it up, let me say a quick word about finger-pointing. People seeking grants are often solving problems, and problems have causes. You can't talk about poverty, spousal abuse, illness, or other serious tribulations without acknowledging that in many instances one component of dealing with the problem is eliminating its cause.

That's true. But in your summary you need to use positive language to draw the reader in (you can get to the tougher stuff in the body of the LOI or in your full proposal if you're invited to submit one). Because you have to be so concise, and you might not know exactly who is reading your letter of inquiry, err on the side of being more positive by focusing on what you'll be doing rather than on who is to blame. For example:

"The Safe Soccer League's 'Yellow Card Project' will in only three years protect more than 400,000 of our youth from the risks of poisoning, at a cost of less than 50 cents per child."

Okay, you have constructed that excellent summary, which will be as long or as short as required by your careful reading of the funder's LOI requirements. Now you have to write the body of the piece. This isn't easy, but it is easier than many tasks in fundraising.

Unlike the summary of your work, which needs to be specially thought about and written, the body of your LOI can be a boiled-down version of your proposal – in some respects, it can function like an outline of your full-bore proposal and budget.

Unless the funder has special requirements, such as a list of questions or even a form to fill out, you simply need to fit your project description into the space permitted. For many, this can be done by taking the outline of your proposal (you did write the proposal from an outline, didn't you?) and fleshing it out into the space allowed, taking special care with ensuring smooth transitions between elements. When I think of the ideal text of an LOI, I picture one of those soft-serve ice creams with a curly top. It just slides down, smooth, cool, and easy.

Before closing out this chapter, let me offer one last piece of advice. Take a Post-It note and write on it, "My goal is to have a proposal invited." Stick the note on your computer and refer to it often.

Every single word in your letter of inquiry needs to be held up to this test and this test only. Don't use the LOI to make grand-scale points about the state of the world, show your erudition or wit, or argue the fascinating minutia of soccer field care.

Single-mindedness in LOI writing is no vice; your only goal is to get that call from the foundation staff person asking for more.

With that admonishment in mind, let's move now to the fun stuff: writing the proposal that results in a grant.

CHAPTER 3

Meat and Potatoes: Proposals and Budgets

Today is deadline day at the foundation. Although a handful of people have sent in their proposals early (undoubtedly the same ones who sat in the first row in junior high), on this day the FedEx man is wheeling a cart to haul the incoming stack of proposals.

I've seen this scenario many times, by the way. Deadline day at a foundation can indeed trigger Christmas-like tactics on the part of suddenly taxed delivery services, although increasing consent from funders to send proposals via the Internet is lessening the pile of papers for everyone.

Eventually, every proposal finds its way to the desk of a program officer. There she sits, a mug of coffee in hand to combat the dreaded occupational disease of program officers: MEGO. The term refers to a condition caused by reading scores if not hundreds of proposals in a brief span of time: My Eyes Glaze Over.

As a proposal writer, know that your first and main

job is to avoid inducing an acute case of MEGO. Your goal is to motivate that program officer to assign a code to your proposal that keeps it alive in the evaluation and screening system. At this stage, you should have no other goal.

After several decades of poring over proposals, I want to share some overall tips with you, before we drill down to specifics.

1) *Present solutions, not problems.* The old conventional wisdom had a proposal starting with a "problem statement." Although many organizations are indeed trying to address serious problems, I've seen far too many proposals that are almost all problem statement, with scant information about exactly what the applicants are going to do to remedy their respective organizations' major concerns. The key here is to inspire with a vision and impress with a credible action plan.

2) *Write clearly.* Unless you're seeking funding for a technical project such as scientific research and are certain the reader of the proposal will understand what you're talking about, avoid jargon and technical terms. Similarly, use metaphor sparingly – save the purple prose for that novel chronicling your fundraising angst.

Use statistics like cayenne pepper: a little goes a long way. If you must go into six pages of detailed charts on some statistical trend, and the foundation's rules permit it, put that wonky stuff into the appendix, so you don't give the reader good cause to give up reading in the middle. Keep the words flowing: short sentences that draw the reader in are usually best.

3) *Don't threaten the funder.* Years ago, during the height of the Cold War, I received a proposal from a major East Coast university asking for $10,000 to fund a conference of academics to talk about the possibility of nuclear war. Although I was sympathetic to the issue of preventing global annihilation, and even then $10,000 wasn't that much money, I didn't see the point of a group of scholars sitting around for a couple of days wringing their hands. There was no action component in the proposal other than jawboning. So I politely declined and forgot about it.

Several weeks later, my phone buzzed and I was told the president of this university was on the line. He was a distinguished scholar with a worldwide reputation. Having totally forgotten about my five minutes with his school's proposal, I took the call and began by inquiring after his health. He wasted no time, retorting, "Mr. Teitel, there will be global thermonuclear war, and it will be your fault." Click.

Although not as colorfully, many proposal writers make the same mistake of thinking that blackmail or guilt is the route to a foundation's checkbook. They think emotional manipulation is an effective tool. I want to tell you emphatically that it isn't. Don't avoid a concise description of the real problems and issues in the world, but don't lay responsibility for fixing the problem at the feet of the funder, either. It won't help you get money.

4) *Focus on what you're already achieving and how*

you plan to continue. Over many years, I've learned to spot proposals that correlate with successful work. Instead of telling me that if our foundation doesn't give you money something awful will happen or that if we don't fund you, you might cease to exist, better proposals say: "We're doing something wonderful here, and we're going to do it with or without you. With you, it'll happen faster and better – but it's happening nonetheless. Please join us in this excellent work."

I once heard a panel of venture capitalists talking about how they do their work. And they said exactly the same thing. They can recognize the businesses they should invest in from the same kinds of statements in the organizations' business plans, which function as proposals in the VC world.

5) *Don't bypass the system.* It often happens in the course of your funding research, especially with small or local foundations, that you find you know someone on the board, or someone who goes to church with that person, or has a kid on their soccer team. So you figure, I'm going to use this advantage and go right to that person, because I read in chapter 1 that board members make the funding decisions, not staff.

There are two good reasons to resist this temptation, unless you have specific and concrete information that such an approach is welcome. The first is that foundation boards pay their staff fancy money to buffer them from being hassled. And even though you're exceptionally articulate and charming, you run a serious risk of annoying just the person you hope will end up liking your work. And as for charm, the funding decision is about your organization and its work: you, the fundraiser, are only a vehicle.

The other reason not to do an end run is the risk it creates with foundation staff. I don't actually know anyone who enjoys having a person go over his head. The board member you're chatting merrily with at the party is my boss. It doesn't necessarily make me feel warm inside to know I've been left out of the equation.

If you really do find yourself standing at the soccer sidelines alongside a board member whose kid is on the same team, find a casual way to let the foundation staff know you have that connection, and you're not exploiting it. Keep the foundation staff as allies – that's the surest route to a check.

6) Use the cut-and-paste function in your word processor, but do it skillfully. Although some foundations have application forms and some ask very, shall we say, *idiosyncratic* questions, in general there are only so many ways you can describe your organization and its activities. Given the convenience of word processing software, there is an understandable tendency to delay writing the proposal until a day or two before the deadline, knowing you can load an old proposal and just stitch and glue until you have something that seems to meet the requirements.

Although it's okay to use a basic proposal for all of the variations you need to produce, be careful not to leave out transitions and connective tissue. Conversely, pay attention to repetition and redundancy. Most of us have a natural tendency to mentally fill in those pesky leaps of logic and narrative that can make the difference between a ho-hum proposal and something that compels.

CHAPTER 4

Writing a Wonderful Proposal

Funding proposals vary widely, from ponderous tomes meant to produce millions of dollars of research funds to simple, eloquent pleas for help. I once funded a group that made their request on a postcard.

Still, you can divide most funding requests into five basic components, even though you may need to adjust for individual circumstances:

The *Summary* – something between a paragraph and a page (check the guidelines before you start) that does a masterful job of meeting the Three Cs standard: clear, concise, and compelling.

The *Vision* – known in the Dark Ages as the problem statement, this section describes the issue you're addressing and why it's important you do so.

Strategies and Tactics – this is where the verbs leap off the page. You say *exactly* what you're going to do that will change something in the real world.

Resources – what will support your strategies and

tactics? This section should include every resource: people, money, time, and material. Don't make the mistake of talking only about money, although finances are a major concern.

Fundamentals – this part sometimes resides in appendices or at the end of the proposal, but it's no less important than the other parts. It includes items such as your tax exemption determination letter as well as other bits and pieces that are either required by the funder or you feel confident are welcome, such as a list of your board members, letters of recommendation, and samples of previously successful work.

With that said, let's now look more closely at each of these components.

■ The Summary

Everything we said about writing a summary for a letter of inquiry applies here, but more so.

It's a major mistake to think the word *summary* actually requires you to summarize your work by simply restating it in fewer words. Unnaturally compressed writing is rarely engaging. Instead, step back and think hard about your elevator speech: how would you tell someone about your work in a minute or two? Organizations that use door-to-door or telephone canvassers are usually good at this – they know they need to be complete and also persuasive in the few seconds before the door is slammed.

When I sat down at my desk and started pulling proposals off the stack, I started with the summary. Here is what I was looking for:

1. Key words that I could connect to what my foundation funded.

2. A beginning, middle, and end to the proposed work. That is, is there a logical flow of strategies and resources so that by the end of the project something will have been accomplished that I could see and maybe even measure?

3. Competence: did I get the impression that this was a going concern, a group of people who knew what they were doing and why? Did I smell success?

4. Red flags: signs that there was a problem with the group, the strategies, or the resources. For example, my eye would stop rather quickly at the word *lobbying*, since that can be an issue between private foundations and the IRS. Or I might have paused at an innocent word such as *international*. I knew that would be a fatal flaw with my particular foundation. If someone's summary talked about their excellent work in Sri Lanka, I knew I could stop reading. This is where foundation staff identifies those that didn't read the guidelines.

This might be a good place for me to mention presentation. Rules for résumés apply here: avoid cute fonts, tiny margins, colorful papers, and binding methods that stymie attempts to file or photocopy your work. Keep it simple, dignified, and accessible – make it easy for the funder to love you. If you send a proposal by e-mail, use a standard format (PDF or Microsoft Word).

■ The Vision

Most proposals, after the summary, tell the reader what the grant-seeking group is working on and why. This is your chance to soar – to wax compelling and to show you know your stuff. In this section, three problems tend to surface, all of which you can easily avoid.

The number one flaw is that people go on far too long about the problem. My theory is that proposal writers care deeply about their work and want to make sure you share their sense of urgency. So they go on and on and on. Think of a brand-new father and his seventy-two pictures of baby Ashley. Instead, go for quality. Select narrative elements that tell your story in a vivid way – not flowery or overly dramatic, just persuasive. Let good, clear, strong words work for you. Quantity doesn't indicate consequence. Windiness more likely leads straight to MEGO.

The second common difficulty in talking about the vision is that people often neglect to say why the issue is important to them. The reasons seem so self-evident to dedicated souls that they don't say it. Never lose an opportunity to explain why people in your organization are involved: connect vision and motivation. This is a key point of selling.

For example, if I'm writing a proposal for the Committee to Reduce Non-Stick Cookware, you might not know from our goal of decreasing non-stick items whether we're idiosyncratic chefs, people concerned about the possible health effects of non-stick coatings, or folks who know that out-gassing from overheated non-stick pots and pans can be fatal to pet birds. If the foundation I'm approaching has a funding category covering animal health, then making sure to say that my organization is composed of bird lovers links our group's vision to the foundation's purpose.

The third pitfall in writing about your core issues is actually a tough one. You need to talk clearly about what you're trying to change but not drown the reader in an abyss of negativity and despair. If you're dealing with one of the many difficult and possibly even horrible issues in our world, then you should say so. Be clear and don't pull punches. But avoid wallowing and redundancy.

Going back to the days of possible nuclear confrontation between the United States and the Soviet Union, one "peace" proposal I read included stark detail of the effects of nuclear explosions, including two pages of melting eyeballs and burning flesh. Tucked in at the end were some general statements about the need for people to pay attention to this danger. There was no proffered hope, no vision of a world that was improved and what it might look like, and very little about how we might actually get to a better place.

This is why I try to avoid the term *problem statement* and instead focus on *vision*. Give the reader some reason to feel hopeful and positive; provide him or her with concrete indications that you're a problem solver, not just a problem describer.

■ Strategies and Tactics

People hate this part, and I don't blame them. If you aren't the shy type, stand on a street corner and ask passers-by what the difference is between a strategy and a tactic. It isn't intuitive for most people. Yet every group asking for money has a strategy, and every group uses tactics to make that strategy work. If you don't say what those things are in your proposal, you risk confusion, and you might be passing up a significant place to connect with your prospective funder.

A *strategy* is the way you mobilize resources to achieve your goals. *Tactics* are the things you do with your mobilized resources. Let's look at an example.

If your organization is concerned about the plight of homeless people in big cities in the winter, your strategy might be to intervene directly in cold weather. Your tactic might be to send around volunteers in vans to bring people indoors and also to pass out blankets.

Strategies are always choices.

Another group concerned about homeless people might use a different strategy: they might work with those in city hall to achieve more funding for services for the homeless. Another organization might provide food, and another might try to change the housing laws so that people don't end up on the street in the first place.

If I'm a funder with guidelines that say I want to support organizations working on homeless issues, I need to know your strategy. Otherwise, I can't tell you apart from the other groups, or it might appear to me that you're rhetorical and unfocused, so I won't want to give you money. Don't hide your (strategic) light under a bushel.

Connect your strategy to your *vision* with an iron chain. Your vision statement is your declaration of values. It says what your organization cares about and thinks is important. On the other hand, your strategic statement tells your organization, its constituency, and your funders how you're going to work to make those values tangible in the real world.

Be careful here to make your case without disrespecting others who make different strategic choices. I've seen far too many comparative sentences in proposals, such as "Unlike those local groups with a Band-Aid approach, like giving out blankets night after night, our organization is working to root out the underlying causes of homelessness in our city." The prospective funder might have just made a huge grant to those you're criticizing. Change in the world usually comes about when people with different strategies work on a difficult problem from many angles in a cooperative way – and funders know this.

Just as your strategy should flow from your vision, your tactics should be a natural consequence of your strategy. If you're working with city hall to change the rules, then it makes more sense to talk about your deployment of expert advocates in the civic process, not the blankets you pass out. Keep it logical, because you're aiming for that light bulb moment when the funder looks up from your proposal and says, "Oh, now I get it!"

■ Resources – Non-Monetary

We'll get to the budget in a moment, because that's everybody's focus. But make sure you account for *all* the resources you'll be deploying in your work. I'm impressed when a group says, "We have a staff of three that represents a total of forty-six years of experience in this field." I take notice when a group working to change the laws about health care has two doctors, an insurance company executive, and three street-level health care advocates on its board. Those are resources.

I also look for reasonable use of resources. If you have three staff and are aiming to make a major change in the way things are throughout the state of Texas, I'm going to raise my eyebrows when your time line promises results in six months.

Showing all the resources and how they'll be efficiently used impresses and indicates good planning. For example, the organization passing out blankets to homeless people on cold nights might have two staff, but it can show an ongoing roster of eighty-eight volunteers. Mentioning only the two staff members raises the question of how the work could possibly get done, whereas discussing the eighty-eight volunteers demonstrates a well-organized effort that is embraced by members of the public.

Keep everything connected: your tactics should be entirely supported by your use of resources. No funder should read a proposal and say, "How are they ever going to do that?" Inventory all of your resources – the people, the material you might have, the time you spend on your work, community support, and less tangible factors such as artistic creativity or a history of strong community good will.

■ Resources – Monetary

And then there's money.

The first part of a good money plan explains how you're going to secure the financial resources to accomplish your task. As with the other elements of your plan, this part of your proposal should connect clearly to your vision and your strategies and tactics.

If you claim strong community support for your work with homeless people in cold weather, one measure of this claim is your large number of volunteers. Another is your ability to show that you have three hundred contributors in your community. Although the dollar amount is important, what best supports your claim of community involvement is how many people from your community are engaged with your cause. Say so.

Even though you're approaching a foundation, be sure to indicate how you'll secure all of the non-foundation resources necessary to propel your work forward. A good program officer wants to locate her niche in your funding ecology. Many otherwise good proposals leave out this information, leading a program officer to suspect that the work will fail because of insufficient resources.

You might say, "We're able to keep going with our base of three hundred supporters in the community, our annual auction, and our cookie sales. But experience has shown that the number of people who spend the winter on the street is increasing by 10 percent per year, while our fundraising efforts grow only by 4 percent per year, which is usual for small community groups of our type. Therefore, we're adding a component of funding from local companies which we think can help us raise half of the shortfall, and we're looking to our local foundation community to make up the rest."

I'm sure you see the strength of this kind of statement. It shows you have a solid base, you have a reasonable plan that appears to have been researched and thought out, and your request of the foundation is both appropriate and compelling. Here is a chance for the funder to make a measurable difference by joining and enhancing your success.

The second part of the money plan is your budget. Start with a scrupulous reading of the foundation's guidelines and do exactly as they say. Foundations are financial institutions and often are picky about money and how it's accounted for. Aside from compliance with the foundation's budget format, be sure to cover absolutely everything. Don't permit the program officer to say, "Well fine, but where in the budget is the cost of those blankets they're passing out?" List donations, in-kind contributions unless the foundation says not to – show how you're budgeting for every single penny.

If your proposal is for $14.5 million a year for five years for cancer research, then you'll probably have plenty of pages of professionally prepared spreadsheets. But I doubt many such people are reading this book.

A typical nonprofit trying to show how the money will be spent should appear professional and on top of the money but also be clear, legible, and organized in ways that make sense to an ordinary person.

Presentation matters a lot in spreadsheets and budgets – MEGO sets in early. Use notes and explanatory sections sparingly, because you don't want to appear defensive. But do explain what isn't self-evident.

And now the secret trick in preparing budgets for foundations. Commit this dictum to memory:

Many foundation boards have a person on them, often the treasurer, who whiles away the long boring parts of the board meeting by checking your math. I can always spot this person because she or he uses a pencil, never ink. And all too often the labor of these math checkers is rewarded. You do *not* want your proposal to fall into this category. Check. Your. Math.

I'm not unsympathetic: I picture you, late at night, having spilled coffee into your computer keyboard for the second time, and your back aching. You've changed the numbers in your budget eleven times. So you slip up a little. No blame, right?

Wrong. Fast-forward six months to the board meeting, where the treasurer is thundering, "You expect us to fund these people who aren't even competent enough to add a simple column of figures? Forget it!" You've killed your funding chances for a dumb reason, and, to make matters worse, you've made your principal ally, your program officer or foundation executive director, look foolish. Not a sterling move as a grant seeker.

Yet it happens again and again. Budgets that don't add up are a common problem.

I said there were three things to your money section: first an overview and context about how you'll secure money to carry out your work, second a budget. The last is something that's a bit difficult to present: a concrete plan for what you'll do if you don't raise your budget.

This is a touchy subject, because it's hardly a hallmark of good selling to dwell on failure. But you simply must be prepared with a cogent answer to the question "What will you do if you can't raise all the money in your plan?" I asked this question countless times and was frequently met with a deer in the headlights look.

Here is why you need to think about this sad topic. First of all, foundation board members love this question. They look at the fact that your budget is $500,000 and you only can account for $300,000 in fairly secure income. So they want to know: Is your organization a going concern? And if they do make a grant, but all the money isn't there, will the foundation's money have been wasted?

A related issue is that the foundation, either at the

staff or board level, might be hard pressed for money, which, believe it or not, happens a lot. We might sit down at a board meeting and know we have about $2 million to spend during this particular funding round. But we might have $3 million in excellent proposals sitting before us.

We can just rank them in order of preference and draw a line when we run out of money. But often funders will attempt to reduce the amount granted to many of the groups on the grounds that some money is better than none.

Assuming you agree that you'd rather have less money than none at all, be prepared to help out, but don't volunteer this information – wait to be asked. If you need $30,000 to round out the budget for your blankets for the homeless work and the foundation staff says, what if you only got $20,000, you shouldn't cry, say you will go out of business, or declare that you'll wing it.

A good answer might be "We could still make good use of the reduced amount by eliminating one delivery crew to save overhead and asking our other volunteers to work an extra hour per night. And we'd also hope to make up the money from local stores and companies." Rehearse this answer; be ready. I can always tell when someone is faking it, and my purpose in asking it isn't to harass but to help – yet I can't do much good with an incoherent or unconvincing response.

■ Fundamentals

When it comes to compiling proposal end matter, Hamlet had it right: "Use all gently." As I've stressed elsewhere, I suggest you first check with the foundation's specifications before adding goodies to your proposal package.

My guess is that grant seekers work on this part of the proposal when they're the most tired, and maybe rushing to meet the FedEx deadline. Thus my staff made phone call after phone call asking applicants to supply their IRS tax determination letter, even though I don't know of a single foundation that doesn't require it.

By the same token, some organizations include thick bundles of testimonial letters. I read one occasionally, but in general I viewed reference letters as an unnecessary assault on our tree supply, since I doubt fundraisers would include letters from those who think the group does a bad job. It's like getting a reference from your mother: nice, but a little predictable.

News clippings fall somewhere in the middle. You're unlikely to include clippings about the indictment of your group's treasurer. Still, a press account sometimes illustrates your competency in a project that relies on public education or demonstrates you have indeed plowed new ground, when pioneering new ground is one of the objectives of your work.

As for your board of directors, list them unless the funder tells you not to. And include unusual or interesting illustrations of your success. These examples will be strongest when you can link your track record to your proposed new work. It can be quite compelling for you to say, "The proposed senior citizen housing program on the Gulf Coast described in this proposal builds on our award-winning reconstruction of 78 houses in the Lower Ninth Ward of New Orleans, following the Hurricane Katrina disaster."

Overall, use the same standard that has permeated this chapter: include anything that strengthens the connections among the various elements of your proposal as well as items that add to the proposal in a specific, concrete manner. Leave out puffery and irrelevancies. When in doubt, don't.

Before we close this chapter, I have one final item and some last cautions to share.

More and more funders are concerned about metrics, that is, specific measurements of outcomes. Many dedicated people bridle at this requirement, fearing that quantifying their work omits the high quality they achieve. They want us to see that not only do they pass out an average of 190 blankets each cold night to homeless people but they also make these individuals feel less isolated, less hopeless, and more connected to other human beings.

Most certainly, tell how your work will improve the lives of others. But in addition, show how you'll measure the impact. If yours is a group trying to change state laws that lead to homelessness, you can say, "We'll know we have succeeded if one of the four homeless services bills pending in the legislature passes within the next two years. And we will count contact hours with members of the state legislature, and show a 25 percent increase in the number of articles that mention our work."

One group that my former foundation funded with a multi-year, multi-million-dollar grant gave me a proposal that showed 57 separate planned outcomes and how each would be measured. Although reporting 57 outcomes on a spreadsheet is a bit extreme, it shouldn't be too difficult for you to predict three or four solid outcomes in your proposal and then be absolutely sure to account for them in your reporting.

As you pause to stretch your weary fingers and tired back from laboring over your proposal, bring yourself back to the reason you're doing your work. Connect with the core motivations and passions that keep you at it, day after day. Then pour that dedication, commitment, and hope for a better world into every syllable of your proposal. When you're done, sit back and know that you've done all you could.

CHAPTER 5

Sweaty Palms: In-Person Meetings with Funders

I am a great believer in shoe-leather philanthropy. Those in the granting field can learn much by leaving the abstract world of proposals and meeting the people who are seeking funds. And for me, anyway, meeting grantees is the most fun a grant maker can have.

In this chapter, we're going to cover the two most common kinds of grant seeker–funder interactions: visits to funder offices, and site visits.

Although it's possible to receive a grant without ever meeting the funder, and many grantees would be happy to avoid the stress and possibly tricky questions emanating from an in-person conversation, there are good reasons to have that meeting.

First of all, some funders can't really get comfortable with a prospective grantee or a new idea until they've interacted beyond the piles of paper. Basically, all you need to do in a meeting is explain yourself. And count yourself fortunate when you have a chance to do so, since the alternative may be the funder tossing your proposal into the dreaded tall pile.

Second, there are some ideas and facets of nonprofit work that have to be seen to be appreciated. Funders and grant seekers don't always agree on which projects these might be. We'll get to that point a little later.

And finally, some grant makers are required to meet people they fund, so you really won't have a choice.

If you want to meet with a funder, here is Rule #1: Do. Not. Ever. Call. The. Funder. At. Home. If this seems obvious to you, my all-time record for outrageous, manners-impaired behavior is held by the man who called me at home at 7 a.m. – on Thanksgiving morning.

He was in town, kind of bored visiting his parents I think, and wanted to know if he could drop by. I admit this is a rather extreme example, but over the years a number of grantees felt perfectly fine contacting me at home, and more than a few appeared on my front porch.

I've thought about this, and I'm just not able to come up with any reason for a person ever to penetrate the professional-personal barrier uninvited.

The second rule, again obvious, is about something that happens all the time. Don't give the funder short notice (fifteen minutes or even a week) that you want a meeting. Leaving aside my internal book of manners, it's simply impractical to expect a busy person to find meeting time on limited notice.

This is one that used to happen to me almost every month: I'd get a call from someone who said he was "in town" and could he come by. Usually, my answer was no, even if it was someone I wanted to meet. Think about it – do I want to hand over tens or hundreds of thousands of dollars to someone who demonstrates that he's not able to manage a simple calendar?

I won't belabor the other obvious rules, such as don't show up without an appointment, don't arrive late, and don't venture to the offices of a foundation in a high-rise in New York in tattered jeans and a T-shirt (none of these examples is made up). In general, what it comes down to is: make a shining impression of your organization, and you'll be just fine.

■ Visiting the Funder's Office

Now let's look more closely at the dynamics of visiting funders in their offices.

It may well happen that a foundation you've applied to will contact you, asking you to come in for a meeting. The only possible answer to this request, unless you're holding a winning lottery ticket, is yes. You might be slightly flustered. After all, thousands if not tens of thousands of dollars could be at stake. So here is a checklist of issues to raise – you don't want simply to book the date and time – if it's possible to stay on the phone a bit longer.

You should ask, "What's the purpose of the meeting?" Finding out what the funder wants to know is vitally important. The response might be that she wants to have a general conversation about your proposal, but she might have something more specific in mind, such as going over your budget, and it would be nice to be prepared.

Your second question is "Who should come to the meeting?" If you're in a small organization, you might want to bring a board member or a community representative. Or, on the other end of the scale, if yours is a big group that works in a technical area or in science, you might want a staff scientist or other expert to accompany you. Usually a huge delegation is a bad idea, but sometimes more than one person can strengthen your hand.

I've met with volunteers, board chairs, and community people over the years who have really impressed and sometimes moved me. It doesn't hurt to ask about including others, if the funder isn't far away and if your bank account can accommodate a bit of travel.

Once the meeting has been arranged, confirm it a week in advance. I remember receiving an e-mail from a grantee who at my invitation was coming from another state. She reconfirmed the date and time, mentioned who was coming, listed the things they hoped to discuss, and politely invited us (there were two people from my foundation in the meeting) to mention any other concerns we'd like addressed. Her e-mail created the meeting's agenda, and the grantee did a good job of maintaining control of the gathering without making me feel overpowered. Perfect.

Okay, so the time comes and there you are in the foundation waiting room. What is in your hand? And, no, I don't mean a briefcase. The only correct answer is: something to hand the funder that he hasn't seen before.

Not another proposal, unless that's the stated purpose of the meeting. And be wary of gifts – most foundation people feel a bit uncomfortable picturing the perp walk when they're indicted for taking bribes. (If you're a local group that has T-shirts and caps, that might be okay, or perhaps a cookbook your organization has produced.) What will suffice is a literature packet in a nice folder – maybe some newsletters and other publications. Just don't show up empty handed. It's poor sales behavior to do so.

In many respects this meeting is a dress rehearsal for the board meeting: in this case you're playing the part of the foundation staff person and the staff person is the board member, asking probing questions. It isn't easy to generalize about meetings with funders because the ones I've been in (from both sides of the transaction) vary. But some aspects of the meeting are fairly common. You're in the funder's offices for two reasons.

First, you want to give the foundation staff an opportunity to look you over. You want them to see that you're competent, that you know your stuff. You put a face on the proposal, give a voice to the issue.

Second, you're there to provide information for the staff person to use in figuring out if she wants to take your proposal on – or later in the game, how she might handle your proposal in her board meeting.

Once you're seated and have exchanged the usual pleasantries, always begin with the same question: "Do you have some things you'd like to cover about our proposal, or would you like me to start with some brief remarks about our work?"

There is a power dynamic here, and this question handles it. You take the initiative in framing the meeting in terms of the funder's needs, not yours. If you blather on before the funder gets to ask his list of questions, it may be time to leave, and you will have missed a perfect opportunity to fill in the blanks and correct misconceptions. If the foundation staff person doesn't begin with questions, then you should give a presentation consisting of three parts.

First, give a brief summary of your proposal, a sort of verbal LOI. There might be someone in the room who hasn't read your proposal, and in any event you want to refresh the memory of those who may have read twelve other proposals that morning.

Second, describe anything that's new. Explain that you're updating the proposal since it was submitted and offer to send this information in writing or even – please forgive me for saying this – rewrite the proposal. Unless you are meeting the day after the proposal arrived in the foundation's offices, you should always include an update – everyone likes to feel she has the most current information.

Third, offer to discuss or clarify any points in your

project that the funder is interested in. You are gently working here to elicit what the funder feels is weak or controversial about your proposal. You're looking to provide answers, not hold a debate.

It isn't advisable to ask if the funder likes or favors your proposal, or if he's going to recommend it. When people feel pushed, they tend to push back, which is just the dynamic you want to avoid. Assume your proposal has some life for that staff person; why else would you be in his office?

■ Site Visits

More rarely, the funder will come to see you. It's too bad site visits are so infrequent, because we funders learn best out of our offices. When you get that call or e-mail announcing a visit, follow the suggestions above – try to pinpoint who's coming, what they want to get out of the meeting, and who in your organization they want to meet with.

Yes, do discard that stack of empty pizza boxes, but don't stress your staff with your nervousness or make them all dress as if they're going to the prom. Confirm the meeting and, once again, be ready with that packet to hand to the funder as part of your greeting.

If, as is sometimes the case, a meal is involved, you might be asked to suggest a local restaurant. Be prepared with a few choices, which you can describe in diplomatic terms, such as, "There's a good basic local seafood place two blocks away, and an Italian place around the corner that has white tablecloths at lunch."

Most people who are picking up the tab appreciate having the price range flagged in advance. And speaking of the tab, I know that some of my esteemed colleagues operate with different standards than I did, but in most cases, it is the putative funder who pays. You might offer to pick up the check if you feel that's called for, but don't insist.

Also, be cautious about who comes to the meal. I was once at an organization's office in New York City and mentioned it was lunchtime. The two people I was meeting with said great, and promptly invited all the employees, seventeen of them, to join us. Leaving aside what that meal did to my budget, I didn't get any actual work done during the confusing and raucous meal ... to the group's detriment.

Assuming your organization runs programs or services, most funders will want to see what they might be funding. Over the years, I've met cowboy poets, participated in street demonstrations, cooked meals for homeless people, and collated mailings with volunteers. One of the great blessings of my work has been meeting the people who dedicate their lives to helping others, often around kitchen tables or in dilapidated walk-up offices.

One big mistake grant seekers make is muting the power and passion of their work. Granted, taking a funder into the community means you can't control what happens. Someone may say something embarrassing. But funders are adults and can handle the unexpected. I know that time and again I've fallen in love with groups because they let me meet their volunteers or those whom they serve.

Let me, in closing this chapter, suggest two ideas to help you induce funders to meet with you. I regret I don't have more.

First, make the offer to come by and meet the funder, or invite her to visit with your organization. Do this even if you don't want to, or you doubt the funder will accept.

A polite invitation can't hurt, most especially in the context of acknowledging a letter that says that your letter of inquiry has been accepted and you're being invited to submit a full proposal. Just make sure your invitation is clear and brief. And send only one. E-mail is best for this kind of task, since so many foundations have watertight phone screening systems, but a phone call could be okay if you think it'll accurately and quickly reach the intended party.

The second technique that worked with me was to illustrate what a site visit might look like. In these days of $69 color printers, you can easily produce a letter showing the smiling faces of your volunteers or the beautiful setting around your program's field office or shots of those who benefit from your efforts. A few times when I was wavering about a visit, framing this picture in my mind helped to tip the balance in the grantee's favor.

CHAPTER 6

Making Sausage: How Foundation Staff and Boards Decide

Once quite a few years ago I was asked to guest-staff a foundation board meeting, while the person whose regular job it was took a break. I knew little about these funders and was fairly new to the field, but it was a chance to see some money flow to organizations I cared about. I worked for six months preparing a thick notebook – often called a *docket* in the foundation trade – that carefully supported my grant recommendations.

On the Saturday of the board meeting, I flew to a distant city, where I was met by a liveried driver and shown to his limousine. He brought me to a large, paneled room in an office building where five businessmen in suits were seated. Each had a copy of the docket notebook in front of him ... unopened.

After introductions, the chairman asked me several general questions about a few of the proposed grants in the notebook. Sixty minutes and $2.2 million later, I was sent on my way.

That's one stereotype of how foundations make decisions, and I've visited with a number that behave similarly. At the other end of the scale are foundations whose boards meet for days at a clip, poring over the details of each and every grant request.

In the face of so much variation, what's a grant seeker to do? In this chapter, we'll look at how foundation staff members prepare themselves for board meetings and how some boards decide what to fund. Our goal is less to study the habits of these strange birds and more to understand how to maximize your chance of getting funded.

■ Foundation Staffing

Most foundations have no staff at all. Often a lawyer or bank trust officer handles the paperwork, or a family member handles things if the foundation represents family philanthropy. But here we're going to focus on those foundations large enough to have professional staff.

Someone – paid staff or bored lawyer – is charged with screening the large number of incoming proposals to select the much smaller number that will receive concerted attention. If you discover you're one of the lucky few who have made the cut, what then?

■ Into the Black Hole

First we have to mention the unpleasant truth that, in many cases, you won't know if your proposal got past the first cursory screening until many months later, when the process for that round of grants has ended. Some foundations, especially larger ones, only send notices *after* the board meets. In some instances, this is because the staff is on a short leash: the board needs to ratify all decisions, even the negative ones.

So take it as a bad omen if there's a thundering silence once you've submitted your proposal. Although I know of instances of grant seekers sending in proposals and receiving a check in the mail, it's not common, because most foundations need to know more about you to make a funding decision.

But say you received a card acknowledging receipt of your proposal and haven't heard anything since. What can you do to find out what's going on, without annoying the person you're hoping will give you money?

Start with a fellow-sufferer. If the foundation publishes a grants list, and if you know or can introduce yourself to someone on that list, call up and ask for advice. You would have been well advised to make contact before you sent anything to the foundation. But even if you didn't, it's not too late to call a colleague and explain that you sent in a proposal but haven't heard anything. She might laugh and say, "Oh, it takes them six months to read anything, don't worry." Or she might have a clue about whom to call and what to say.

If all else fails, call the funder and tell the truth: you sent in your material and are wondering if there's something you can or should do. I can promise you that a person who is paid to answer a foundation's phones continually fields versions of this call.

■ Position Papers and Context Statements

What is the program staffer doing while you pace your office? If he is typical, he's doing several things. One is refining the foundation's grant making by creating position papers. In board meetings, my staff and I took careful note of what our board members said, and some of what we heard turned into exploratory or issue papers.

Let's assume the funder's guidelines have some language about supporting access to health care for all citizens in the state. In the board meeting, a member mentions an article she read about the problem of getting health care to the children of homeless families living in shelters. There's some discussion, including disagreement about what care is already made available and by whom. During a lull in the conversation, I might point out that this discussion is about an issue that fits well within our guidelines, and ask if the board would like to see some staff work on it.

The origin of this kind of staff investigation varies quite a bit. In larger foundations, there's often a formal staff-driven process for determining what will be explored and by whom. These investigations are how foundations learn, how they attempt to keep their guidelines relevant. You as a grant seeker will sometimes learn of the process when out of the blue you get a call from some program officer wanting to ask you about the field you work in. Sometimes funders assemble formal expert panels, but often they just network around.

In addition to these "think pieces," what else is going on inside the foundation? Most likely, the foundation staff members are beginning to shape up their dockets, often using the think pieces as templates. As your proposal rises in the pile, a staff person might give you a call with some points that need clarifying or want to know a few things that didn't appear in your proposal.

■ The Inner Sanctum

Foundation boards vary as widely as the foundations they govern. Some boards consist of family members, spending an ancestor's largess. Others are teams of experts. A number of boards mix and match, including family people, experts, lawyers, even politicians. Private foundations may list their board members on their Web sites and are required to identify their board on their annual IRS returns, Form 990-PF, which are available online.

Scoping out the board can be useful. If your proposal is for funding lab work on anhydrous bisphenol molecules and you learn from your research that the board is composed of weighty chemists, you should write a technical proposal showing off your ability in the field. If you're writing to an ordinary family or non-technical people, put more of your energy into clear and effective communication about issues and solutions. Conversations with previous grantees as well as the foundation's own staff will tell you what to expect.

Once the proposal is in, it's usually too late to make

major revisions, so be sure of the board's makeup before you put fingers to keyboard.

The dynamic between foundation boards and staff is a complex one. The staff has been working full-time on the issues and proposals that end up in front of a board, which perhaps meets once or twice a year. The board's job is to be the keeper of the foundation's mission, to deploy money that best realizes its purpose. Yet in many instances they rely heavily on staff, especially if the board is composed of more general members of the public or a family.

When new staff started at one of the foundations I ran, I made sure to describe how the decision-making process worked, and I think it applies in many foundations. The staff person comes into the board meeting having worked for months on his suite of recommended grants. He's met with prospective grantees. There have been numerous phone calls, perhaps a site visit, and possibly hours of research. The staff person has become an expert – and an advocate.

During the board meeting, good board members will ask questions, poking at the staff with queries designed to find out two things. First, does that staff person really know what she's talking about? The board member wants to confirm that this recommendation comes from someone who has done her homework on the foundation's behalf.

Second, the board member is trying to figure out if the staff person is pushing the foundation into a new direction or otherwise subverting the guidelines. Many board members see their primary role as being guardians of the vision of the foundation, so they're diligent in making sure that some aspect of a proposed grant won't be derailing the organization from its tracks.

Under the best of circumstances, this dynamic between the board and staff can keep a foundation healthy and competent. Under other circumstances, the decision-making process can slide into debate and even, as I have witnessed, shouting, table pounding, or tears.

Staff can become frustrated with what they perceive as board members who resist change or who misunderstand. Board members may see staff as promoting outsiders rather than supporting the board's decision making. Frequently board members will grumble that they're not paying staff to hassle them.

For the decades I ran foundations, I had a rule with my staff during board meetings: I asked them to sit where they could see me, and to look at me frequently, however painful that may have been.

In the process of give and take with board members, it's understandable that sometimes the staff gets carried away in "explaining" the proposed grant. When this happened, we had subtle signals to help each other. Mine was a near-imperceptible shake of my head. If that didn't take *immediate* effect, I'd draw a horizontal line with my finger across my neck. If in the heat of the moment that piece of subtlety was ignored, I'd interrupt.

My invariable rule has always been that when the board

is apparently deciding not to make a grant, staff must instantly stop endorsing the proposal.

An important dynamic of a foundation board meeting is that, despite their months of concentrated work, staff should be ready to toss proposed grants overboard – without hesitation. Staff members who persist in pushing grants the board doesn't want to make are usurping the board's power, and they're sometimes shown the door.

The crucial message for a grant seeker is that you should help foundation staff members prepare to be your best surrogate. But staffers know who pays them; their advocacy on your behalf has definite limits.

■ Singing for Your Supper

Some foundations invite those with pending proposals to make presentations directly to the board. Years ago I myself received such an invitation. I awoke before dawn to drive through morning traffic to a nearby city for my big day, with $330,000 riding on my performance. No pressure.

In the early morning darkness I failed to see a pothole just as I was taking a sip of my coffee. The front of my shirt was instantly drenched. At the next exit, I drove off the highway to find a replacement while praying I wouldn't be late for my 9 a.m. meeting. I still have the polyester shirt I was able to locate in a variety store that was just opening. It's a good reminder of what grantees go through that funders don't even dream of. I called that garment my "$330,000 shirt."

If you're invited to appear before a board, aside from

being careful with spills, you should question the foundation's staff carefully in advance, then do exactly and precisely what they tell you. Staff members have a strong interest in your doing well and making them look good. If they say, cover your three objectives in four minutes, don't talk about something else for five. Here are other general guidelines for in-person interactions with foundation boards:

1) Take exactly the amount of time you're given, no more and no less. Practice until you can do it right.

2) Be polite but not gushy. Obsequiousness isn't conducive to a dignified impression.

3) If you're asked questions, answer succinctly and honestly. Arguing with foundation board members is only advised if your proposal is for support of Self-Destructors Anonymous.

4) Stay on the subject at hand, and only pass out materials that staffers have told you are welcome.

5) If you're asked to a meal, eat beforehand and just pick at your plate. This will allow you to bestow your charms liberally on those around you, rather than wasting time tucking into the free food or being asked a question just as you fill your mouth with au gratin.

Once the foundation board has met, all you can do is wait.

■ The Denouement

At some point, you'll find out what happened to your funding request (a phone call is probably good news).

Many foundations, once they've announced you're slated to receive funding, will send a packet with instructions about grant compliance and reporting that you must fill out to receive the check.

For reasons I cannot fathom, there are a few grantees in every funding round that don't return the paperwork. You train for years, run that Olympic race, win, and then don't show up for the gold? This delay can be a problem for funders who are making grants at the end of their fiscal year and need to have the check in your account by a certain date. Don't look like a flake: read the paperwork carefully, get the signatures you need, and send the package back.

Unfortunately, things might turn out the other way. Even after you've done everything just right, when you know your work is the very best, when you stayed up several nights rewriting your proposal to suit the funder's unorthodox requirements, you might still get turned down. It hurts.

If you have any kind of relationship with the foundation's staff, you might place a call, thank them for their presumed effort on your behalf, and ask if they can share anything that would shed light on the outcome. I advise you to use something close to my language here: be gentle, succinct, then get off the phone.

You might well be able to learn something, make a few changes, and try again. You might be able to have that staff person tell her colleague across town when she calls about your new proposal that you're a good person to work with. At all costs, avoid arguing or castigating. It isn't conducive to building the kind of relationship that produces future funding.

CHAPTER 7

Reports: What to Do After You're Funded

After you've been told the fabulous news about your grant award, and the champagne has fizzled in your coffee mugs, I recommend you do three things:

1. Sit down with a tasteful piece of stationery or cheery card and send a thank you note to the funder. You don't need to gush or grovel, but a hearty thanks is one of the ways to cement your new relationship. Have a board member sign, or have all the staff in your small office write something, or some other token of genuine appreciation. Even an e-mail is ok, but just do it.

2. Put the funder on your mailing list – *judiciously*. What you don't want to do is behave like the funder's kids – you cash the check and aren't heard from again. And you want to avoid the funder looking at your material eleven months hence and saying, "Who?"

Instead, gently and with restraint keep your group in front of the funder. Maintain that feeling of connectedness and create the impression that you're all in this together.

If you have a monthly or quarterly newsletter, put the funder on the list for a free lifetime subscription. I don't actually think the funder should have to pay extra for information, but one group we funded with over three-quarters of a million dollars did indeed charge us $25 for their materials. We live in a diverse world.

If your organization holds events, and the funder is local, make sure she's invited. Don't expect her to attend, but people like to feel included, and events illustrate your group's activities.

3. Take an empty file folder, label it "foundation reports," and place it on your desk. As successes or interesting events in your organization are documented, remember to slip a copy into that folder. News clippings are an obvious choice, as are attractive invitations to events, and concise reports to your own board.

When it comes time to report on a grant, reach into this file, go back twelve months in what you pull out, and walk to the photocopier.

A major aspect of reporting is financial accounting. There may be some person on the planet who likes this part of the grant-making process, but I haven't met him. Yet this section of the report is central, because if someone gives you publicly subsidized money, you should be willing to show how you spent it.

This is one time when you'll want to suppress every ounce of your creativity and do exactly what the funder says in their reporting requirements. There's a good chance the financial part of the reporting specifications was written by a CPA or a lawyer, and you cross those kinds of people at your peril.

I want to suggest three reasons for paying close attention to grant reporting.

First, most groups hope to receive repeat funding. Those that are late or fail to comply with reporting requirements will be on shaky ground for a renewal grant. And even if you know you're not going to receive a second grant because of certain rules and restrictions, you still have to assume that funders talk to each other, because we do.

So when I run into a colleague and he says he has a proposal from your group and noticed that my foundation used to fund them, you don't want me to say either "Who?" or even worse, "Oh yeah, those folks never reported." Reports are a way of building relationships, and relationships underpin grant making.

Second, you might actually teach the funder something. Let them know how the grant turned out, what was a great success and what was unanticipated; share the lessons. My staff and I used to say we studied at the University of Grantees. In most foundations, the board is interested in how their grants turn out, and they might even enjoy reports, or at least summaries.

Finally, even though some might smirk, I think you can learn from your own reporting. Sitting down and summarizing what you did over the past year is an excellent way to improve your work. It forces you to step back from the daily struggle and think about what you accomplished, what your greatest challenges were, and what you've learned.

And as long as you're going through the trouble of writing the report to comply with grant terms, get some mileage out of it. Share the document with your own board and staff members – give them an opportunity to feel proud, too.

CHAPTER 8

You Really Can Do It

Many years ago I found myself trudging along in a Central American tropical forest with a group of funders and journalists. Our host was a prominent scientist who was conducting fieldwork in the area. As we squatted in a little clearing, taking a break from our hike, one of the journalists asked the famous biologist to explain his success in securing funding over so many years.

The scientist slowly finished folding up his snake-capturing bag, looked over at me, and said, "Oh, funders are like monkeys. You can study their habits and learn to manipulate them."

Guilty as charged. Some days, I wanted to fund everyone.

By the same token, grantees gave me and others in the foundation world a great gift: the opportunity to work all day surrounded by passionate people striving to improve the world around us.

In closing Part I of this book, let me share two final thoughts.

First, the fundraisers I trusted most were the

unassuming non-experts who infected people around them with authentic passion. Don't let the pressure of meeting deadlines and budgets separate you from your dedication. Your commitment is the best tool you have.

Second, don't forget that funders seem important because they control one resource so completely. But in fact, real change in the world comes not from grandiose granting guidelines but from the perseverance and imagination of those trying to penetrate the granting process in order to do good for others. Those are the truly important people. And to them I send my sincerest gratitude and respect.

PART TWO

MYTHS ABOUT FOUNDATIONS

After working for both nonprofits and foundations during the forty-five years since I studied Greek mythology in college, I've seen that there are also myths that bedevil grant seekers and funders.

The stories we use to guide us through the fraught and tortuous path of extracting funding from philanthropies are based on reality, but if we take them too seriously, we'll end up like a deluded modern Achilles who plays in traffic, thinking our magic heel confers invulnerability.

Grant seekers will best be able to endure the slings and arrows of the proposal and granting processes if their eyes are open and their minds clear of the distorting folklore that makes an already tough job even harder.

CHAPTER 9

Myth One

Fundraising Isn't *That* Hard

There may well be people who bounce out of bed and rub their hands together, anticipating with glee another day of writing proposals and cold-calling funders – but I have a feeling there aren't many.

How could there be when, on average, foundations reject half of all proposals they've agreed to consider (some reject as many as 80 percent).

Given the huge amount of effort that's devoted to researching funding sources, collecting project information, creating budgets, writing proposals, and then sending the right material in the right format to the right foundation at the right time, preparing grant applications is (most often) thankless work for an undependable reward. Imagine how quickly the gambling industry would collapse if the average slot machine player had to do all that paperwork to encounter similarly poor odds, instead of simply pushing a button?

Some years ago, when I sat on the grant seeker's side of the desk, I applied to a foundation that began the process by sending me a page of proposal requirements. It included a list of words whose appearance would be grounds for automatic rejection. The exact font and paper type were specified, and I was told the mandated size of the margins down to two decimal places. That's only a sample of what the foundation demanded, not to make a grant, but to *consider* one.

Although that foundation's behavior was extreme, there's no doubt funders often go to some trouble to restrain creativity and autonomy. And for grant seekers this problem is only getting worse. Increasing numbers of funders are using Web-based applications, which further constrain your ability to express yourself.

How do people respond to this system designed to spoil their fun? In my experience, it's often in one of three ways. A common coping mechanism is for grant seekers to pretend that foundation fundraising is, well, fun and they're enjoying every minute of it. Like Tigger, these folks would bounce into my office, loudly jolly about the prospect of hearing, most likely, the reasons why I wouldn't fund them. It was baffling how they thought I'd perceive them as genuine.

A second group is obsequious, sometimes to the point of groveling. They seem to picture themselves as young Mozarts, flattering some count with a powdered wig into parting with a paltry sum to subsidize their genius. Once again my credulity is strained. Not every tie I own is perfect, not every joke hilarious, not every bon mot profound.

The third group, at least more honest, did a great job of getting in touch with their anger, seemingly just on the way to my office. They made sure I saw the weight of their shoulder chip, and would lecture me at some length about how much this whole process of asking for money was beneath them. Their emotional vocabulary seemed to range from condescension to livid invective. I was occasionally called names. Well, it's a change from the soft sell.

I want to be clear: I was the funder with the guaranteed paycheck; I could take whatever Tigger, Mozart, and Attila had to dish out. But did it grease the funding skids? Did these tactics turn me into their passionate advocate before my board? Did I learn what I needed to know to figure out how to help these individuals?

I think not.

A grant seeker owes it to those who depend on her prowess to cast aside personal angst and do what it takes to land the grant. What worked best with me, and I believe many other funders, was a matter-of-fact, professional demeanor. I was most impressed when I felt I was in the presence of someone who was dedicated, competent, and, most of all – a person who got things done. This professionalism includes ignoring personal discomfort with the nature of the process in the service of the greater good – in this case, support of the applicant's worthy project or organization.

Overcoming the intrinsically pessimistic nature of grant seeking is difficult, and many people struggle with it daily. Yet those who can't get past their feelings of unhappiness usually broadcast that fact loudly enough to significantly diminish their prospects for success – talk about a self-fulfilling prophesy. The funder's job does become more fun if yours does, too, but I'm making my plea for more altruistic reasons: people who enjoy their work do a better job; it's as simple as that.

CHAPTER 10

Myth Two

Foundations Are
Straightforward and Honest

Because they more or less have total and unaccountable control over a scarce resource, funders *always* have the advantage. Much that is dysfunctional in grant seeking issues from this power imbalance. Toss in generally weak regulation and scant accountability, and it's not surprising that funders often operate in ways that are unfair and less than straightforward.

It's worth looking at this imbalance, not because it's news, but to identify ways to cope with these problems that don't undermine your goal of winning a grant.

Often when people tell me stories of funder unfairness or deception, I think, "What tales I could tell." For example, I had a foundation colleague who left his job to start a business with twin objectives. He directly managed pools of money for individuals and foundations; at the same time he served as a consultant to funders who paid him to explore new areas for their philanthropy. This fellow's modus operandi was to call nonprofits working in the subject areas he was hired to report on. Dangling before them the possibility of a grant, he'd "assign" these groups portions of his report to write. Few if any people actually received funding. The curious thing is, even after figuring out what was going on, many continued to help this slithery man, in the faint hope he might steer money their way, and also from fear he could become a formidable enemy.

Other examples of funder injustice are less extreme, but more common. They come from aspects of the foundation business that are least legislated and regulated: lack of transparency, few standards of conduct, and, most of all, an endless supply of grant seekers who seemingly will tolerate anything to secure funding. The sheer number of supplicants allows some funders to say, "Fine. If you don't like me, take your grant request elsewhere. Others will fill your shoes."

In recent years, there's been progress in addressing some features of bad behavior. The funder's main trade group, the Council on Foundations, has worked to create and promulgate ethical standards for funders. Reform groups such as the National Committee for Responsible Philanthropy have helped shed light on funder behavior. The more recent rise of statewide associations of nonprofits has provided a safe platform from which grant seekers can speak to funders with a united voice. And a few media outlets have created philanthropy "beats," which provide a mild deterrent to abuses.

But while waiting for funders to clean up their own

act, what can you do about those who aren't straight with you? Let's look at some examples.

I think the largest area of prevarication is in offering you an explanation of why your request was turned down. Second, the most dangerous mendacity is the gap between what the guidelines say and what is really funded. And third, perhaps the most significant aspect of funder unfairness is the skewing of awards toward certain grantees, irrespective of the work the guidelines say is most likely to receive support. Let's examine how these scenarios can play out for you.

You asked for a grant, you may even have been invited to submit a proposal, you worked hard to meet all the criteria, submitted all the documents and attachments, and even so, you were turned down. Okay, we all know that an invitation to submit a funding request isn't a promise, only an opportunity. Still, once you're turned down, what you really want to know is *why* you didn't get the grant.

This information can be important, for if you can learn why you were rejected, maybe you can do something about it, perhaps with this funder in the future or with other sources of support. If you receive the typical anodyne letter, it's my belief you can call your contact to ask why you were turned down. Of course you need to do this in the least confrontational manner – not because I care to shield my well-padded colleagues from your disappointment, but because it's never a good idea to burn bridges. Maybe you'll get a grant someday.

From this call, you may not glean anything useful. If

that's the case, and it frequently is, then your only recourse is to scour the list of awards that *were* made in the granting round that rejected you. Look at the groups closest to yours and try to identify tactical and strategic differences. If that doesn't help, maybe the difference was something in your proposal. Or maybe it was favoritism (we're going to discuss that problem in a minute). If there's no group resembling yours, you should suspect that's your answer right there – the foundation decided not to fund your area, even after encouraging you to apply. That does happen. Boards change their minds.

What about the second perilous area of funder misdirection: the gap between what's espoused and what's actually done? To some extent this is a common problem, like when the entrée brought to you is a little different from what the menu described. Many restaurants don't or can't reprint their menus for what they see as minor alterations to their bill of fare.

Fair enough, but haddock instead of cod doesn't equate to months of focused effort for a six-figure grant that was cast in the wrong light because you naively took the foundation at its word. Regardless of the reason for the gap between theory and practice, what can you do about this problem?

You already know the obvious: look at recent grants, and, if you possibly can, ask a foundation representative to explain the section of the guidelines you're especially interested in. Be sure to ask a specific question – it'll lower the odds of your being told to visit the foundation's

Web site. You might say, "I'm not sure if we'd best fit under the 'Community Improvement' section or the 'Health Effects' granting" – you're asking for a specific choice. Or, "It looks to me like we're in your foundation's statewide initiative grant making, does that make sense to you?"

I have to warn you that some program officers flat out refuse to respond to questions about their guidelines. They fear being blamed if you do what they say and still don't get the grant. I myself recall quite a few instances of advising grant seekers, only to receive angry calls or e-mails when those attempts to help didn't unlock the coffers.

There may be other remedies. For one thing, you could go back several granting cycles in the foundation's funding, note the successful grantees, and try to plot a trend. You might say to yourself, "Now I can see that the rhetoric has stayed constant, but the foundation's granting tendencies are moving away from large-scale strategies toward more locally based work. I'll showcase our community-based efforts in my next proposal."

Last in this list of foundation dodges is the question of playing favorites. Do funders have pet grantees? Absolutely! Some people just plain favor certain organizations for reasons they never reveal. If you're up against favoritism or a grudge – they're pretty much the same thing – I'm going to say something I hope is the only instance of this particular advice anywhere in this book: Give up.

Bias is by definition something you can't put on the table or confront. If you keep losing out to a similar organization because you've learned the funder has a "special" relationship with that group or harbors some impression of you that can't be shaken, walk away. Put your energy where it'll do you some good.

Over many years as a foundation staffer, I worked with countless funders who had the best of intentions and very high standards. Yet I know that in a situation of extensive and largely unaccountable power, even continual vigilance over behavior will sometimes fall short. The grant-seeking process seems dishonest and unfair at times, because it is.

CHAPTER 11

Myth Three

Charming the Foundation Will Conceal Your Flaws

Some years ago I left the foundation world to spend a few years running a nonprofit. The job was great fun, but early on I made the mistake of copying a colleague's technique of calculating how much money I needed to raise each day to meet overhead. Terrified, I stopped most of my program work and became a full-time fundraiser, a fate that awaits many nonprofit execs.

Some of the foundations I called were run by people who only months before had been my colleagues – in some cases, friends. I discovered there were three kinds of reactions from my former associates. One group greeted me instantly and heartily, curious about how I was faring in my new role. I pierced their foundations' screening with ease.

The second group also took my calls. With these people there was palpable awkwardness, a loss of fluency. I felt like I had acquired a long list of "exes." Clearly, my change in status was causing conflict: although they did speak with me, my new situation was creating conspicuous unease.

And, as you have probably guessed by now, the third group stiff-armed me. I generally couldn't get through to them at all, and in one or two instances when I did, I was treated to an arch chill. These funders had moved me from one part of their world schemata to another – quickly and completely. Funder became supplicant.

Let me ask you, in the world of funder ethics – a phrase that might seem ironic – which behavior toward me was most appropriate? Before you quickly condemn the cronies who let me right in and greeted me warmly (perhaps while you were on hold), let's look into what might have been going on.

People seem naturally to start where they're comfortable. And that includes an inclination to speak with those they know and trust. Many of my former colleagues might have been doing me a favor by taking my call, but I'd like to think some accepted contact from me because they saw me as a successful operative.

But what about you? You're not a former funder. How do you get *your* calls returned? A good place to start is by deciding your overall approach, a marketing strategy, if you will. Here's what I mean.

There are a number of ways to sell a product or service. For example, if I invented a revolutionary car that runs on hydrogen, I might run commercials that extolled the special features and unique advantages of my product. My relentless message would be "Save Money. Save Gas. Buy Marty's Car." I'd purchase as much ad space as I could and keep hammering away at variations of this pitch.

But there's another kind of advertising as well. Many ads talk about the wonderful nature or general benefits of a company. They tell us how they don't harm the environment, or how they strive to make the world a better place. Often these ads fail even to mention they want you to buy something.

These two kinds of marketing tell us something important about how you can move from being one more screened-out supplicant to someone whose proposals are read and whose calls are accepted – maybe even someone who's sought out.

The intense demands of grant seeking understandably cause us to shout a version of "Buy Marty's Car." You probably can't ever stop doing that form of marketing. But successful grant seekers often add the second component, the more values-oriented approach, to their bag of tricks. I know individuals whose name on a proposal or a phone message denotes steadiness, reliability, and solid work quality. Moving yourself into the world of foundation trust is closely associated with five traits I want to discuss here.

- *Dependability*

Many nonprofits employ really smart staff with occasionally brilliant ideas, but quite a few of these individuals have spotty records in the accomplishments department. When I read their proposals and thought back to my experiences with them, I knew I couldn't depend on these grant seekers to get the work done, or get it done when promised, or the way they said.

Dependability is more than a personal preference. I funded you to do the work that I told my foundation's board was important and worth putting money into. How and if the work got done was up to you. Which meant, how the directors who employed me viewed the quality of my grant making was in your hands. This is not a small point.

The indirect nature of my profession meant I was going to favor those who I knew delivered, who were on time and under budget. Put negatively, being flaky is grant-seeking death.

A few years ago I made a grant to a large organization for urgent work that looked like a great opportunity. After meeting with the grant seeker and checking on both the idea and the substance of his project, I added it to my board's docket, and the grant was approved.

Once I sent the check, I had a hard time getting the man to return my calls. His interim report, when I finally nagged it out of him, was vague, and because I'm not a total fool, I could see he was in part claiming the work of others as his own. About a year later, the organization's executive director called me up. I was interested to hear from this man, recalling his signature on the contract from that prior grant. He started right off pitching me for a new proposal. I interrupted him and asked about the previous grant, pointing out that I was missing a great deal of information, had been given the run-around, and other items on my list of complaints.

The executive director was somewhat miffed at my recital. He told me that although what I said might be true (might?), the person in question no longer worked there, so it wasn't any concern of his.

Now there's a call I stopped returning.

• *Good Referrals*

Once you received a grant from my foundation, I began to view you as a partner. So if I needed to know about something that I thought you knew more about – not an unusual situation for me – I'd call you up.

Maybe my board was thinking about expanding our grant making. I might have been writing a paper. Or perhaps I'd been tapped for a keynote address. I'd call or e-mail my foundation's grantees before anyone else, because I understood them pretty well, having done the pre-grant investigation. I also thought that since I had helped them secure some funds, they wouldn't mind giving me a few moments. This is what separates entirely appropriate partnerships from the exploitative behavior of the consultant in the last chapter. The individuals I called had already received the grant.

It might surprise you to learn that asking for help from a grantee isn't always a productive experience. Some claimed total ignorance of the other players in their field. Some took my call as an invitation to tout their organization for an additional or increased grant. I had grantees say, "If you have more money available for this work, why aren't you giving it to me?" And on quite a few occasions, grantees responded to my testing of names with sneers and derision.

If a funder – or potential funder – should happen to call you for information, it's a good policy to drop what you're doing and help. There are three reasons for this.

First, here's your chance to demonstrate your knowledge of the field.

Second, you have the opportunity to exemplify that change in the world often comes about from groups of groups, from social movements, from large-scale cooperation. You get to look like a team player. I've called grantees to ask them to speak at a funder conference – normally a treasured chore – and have been told that although they'd be happy to do so, here's the name of someone who's a great speaker and would be better. That's a referrer I remember.

Third, you're presented with a forum to show off what a smart and creative thinker you are. If I'm an investor in your organization or might become one, it can't hurt if you sparkle a bit.

Grantees have taken my thinking in new directions, shown me better ways of framing problems, suggested emerging strategies, and connected me with people I never would have thought of.

• *Publish or Perish*

Being seen as an authority in your field enhances your prospects for a grant. Too often smart people in nonprofit leadership roles told me, "I wish I had time to write, but I have more important things to do."

Maybe so, but publications allow you to put yourself in front of your public, and funders are part of your public. Articles, clippings, and books came across my foundation desk continuously, and those names were more likely to stick in my mind. If you can't make it into the pages of the *New Yorker* or have a book sold by Amazon, you can locate smaller publications hungry for articles. At the very least, you still have your own Web site or blog and your organization's newsletter. The act of publishing is important because you're subjecting your thoughts to the marketplace of ideas; you're willing to be judged by your peers and others. It's an authentic kind of accountability.

• *Speak!*

Similarly, think hard before declining an invitation to address funders, and especially their boards. No one expects you to cancel your daughter's wedding or miss your scheduled trip to Cancun. Yet people sometimes told me they were unavailable because they'd miss a staff meeting; another said he'd have to reschedule lunch with his brother. One nonprofit executive director told me, "I have nothing to say."

Part of good grant seeking, and good leadership, is

sharing your ideas and also being seen as someone who's generous with his or her expertise.

• *Staying Power*

The final quality that helps you break out of the pack is staying power. Although many people, including me, moved jobs from time to time, some seem to flit like hummingbirds. How can they get to know a field in a few months? How can I trust someone who's always a beginner? A six-page résumé isn't always a good sign.

On the other hand, there are grantees I knew for years, a few for decades. They may have moved from organization to organization. But I could readily identify the unifying thread in their work. They knew the issues, the players, the laws and regulations, the community – they just plain knew their stuff. When I contacted them for their views I knew their opinions were built on solid experience and thought.

Once someone in my office referred to one of these grizzled men as "Marty's friend." I was taken aback, because even though I'd seen the pictures on his desk change from chubby babies to soccer players to smart-looking college kids, I didn't really know him in a personal way. I simply understood that this was a guy who knew his field and cared deeply about it, who delivered the goods, and, especially, someone whose name on a proposal was a sign of thorough preparation and meticulous execution. Not actually a friend, but someone to count on.

Years ago, before computers were in wide use, I had a Rolodex card file the size of a Goodyear tire. Someone in my office gave me yellow plastic sleeves to hold the cards I needed to find fast. I often thought that the two dozen or so grantees with those bright sleeves weren't necessarily the best, nor the brightest – but they were the substantial people who would get things done, putting one foot in front of the other for years. There were world changers encased in those sleeves.

CHAPTER 12

Myth Four

Funders Don't Read Grant Reports

There are some people who love reading grant reports, and an equal number who love writing them. They could fill a minivan, I think.

The rest of us struggle with two main misconceptions when it comes to grant reports, one for each party to the funding transaction. Each is based on more than a little truth:

It's another hoop, they don't read them anyway, say the grantees.

Once they've cashed the check, they'll ignore us till they need more money, say the funders.

Let's look first at the grantee misconception. Back when I was in college at the University of Wisconsin, several of my dorm-mates and I had the same freshman English teacher. It didn't take us long to figure out he wasn't reading our weekly assigned papers. Our mandated prose came back with no marks other than a grade, which was invariably an A for everyone. We suspected we couldn't all be that capable, every single week.

One Friday night, as we sat griping about the English paper sullying our prospects for otherwise full-time carousing, we hatched a plan. We agreed to use a common phrase and place it arbitrarily in our papers. We selected "peanut butter" and determined that each of us would insert these as the third (and fourth) words of the third line of the third page, no matter what.

The following week our papers came back to us with the same As, nothing else marked. For the rest of the semester, we gathered each Friday night to select the word of the week. No one ever received any indication that their papers were being read.

More than forty years later, as I read reports from grantees, I wondered if that undergraduate absurdist tradition continues. A few reports were magnificent. More than a few were dreary, and of course quite a few were simply missing.

Some time ago when I was at my desk going through my incoming mail, I came across a report from a grantee I knew was reliable – I'd been watching his efforts for years. As I began reading, something about the report caught my attention.

Then it came to me: there was a clever turn of phrase I'd read before. I thought maybe the writer had used the same description in his proposal. That's okay to do – the report should tell the reader how the proposed work turned out – but I had a funny feeling about this report.

By now you know what's coming. I retrieved the previous year's report and, yes, it was word-for-word the same. It was no clerical mix-up either: all the dates had been changed to match the current year. I then asked someone in my office to dig out the grantee's file from the year prior, and *it too contained the same report.*

For a few days I contemplated the neat stack of identical reports on my desk. "How could I be so stupid?" I thought.

As I debated what to do, I went over the reasons that most funders require reporting, and also what I'd heard from grantees about why they hate reports. Maybe it *was* all a charade. Maybe we could dispense with these reports. Maybe no one would be worse off. But I kept coming back to the three reasons funders demand reports.

First of all, we want to learn and complete the loop. In making the grant, the foundation vetted the proposal and went through the board decision-making process. Finding out what happened to the money allows funders to refine their investigation and decision making. (For clever grantees who use it to reinforce their credibility and competence, the report is also a valuable PR or marketing opportunity.)

The second reason for requiring a report is a legalistic one. The IRS, mother of many foundation procedures, requires reports when funders engage in a process called *expenditure responsibility.* Simply put, this means the funder places the grantee's work under its own IRS tax exemption and is therefore culpable if the money is misspent. I've worked for funders who take expenditure responsibility, and doing so entails a checklist of requirements, including written reports.

In the likely event that a report isn't a legal requirement, it's still legal protection for the grantee. As a lawyer might say, your report gives the grantor "notice." You promised to do certain things in exchange for some money. Having revealed your activities, someone later on would have a difficult time accusing you of nefarious actions. The report helps you to cover your ... grant.

The third reason isn't based on a scientific survey – it's more of an impression I have from meeting hundreds of foundation board members and staff over the years. Some funders feel a report is an essential part of the granting transaction: "I gave you something, now you must give me something in return." This give and take is necessary, as these funders see it, for grant making to be fair and balanced.

Now, confession time. When on the receiving end of grants, I myself occasionally received notices, not terribly different from those I sent to errant grantees, reminding me that a report was overdue. It's hard enough gathering your wits and resources to write a proposal about what you'll do in the future. It's all the more difficult to talk about what you already did when you've moved on to new and more interesting projects.

My second confession is that I'm a recovering report

ignorer. Just as it's boring to write reports, it's boring to read them. And reading reports written by bored writers is almost guaranteed to drop your eyelids.

What might help both parties are two somewhat contradictory trends in grant reporting. One is the move toward form-based reporting – sometimes on the Web and sometimes via paper. Foundation staff use report forms to compare the same answers to the same questions and to show trends and overall change in an issue. They can compare the effectiveness of various tactics and strategies.

For grantees, forms relieve them of having to invent a report. Although originality is constrained by form-based reporting, most of us don't actually look to grant reports as a creative outlet in our lives. For many, it's less painful when they can say, "Just tell me what you want to know, and I'll tell you."

The other reporting trend goes in a somewhat different direction, although both approaches can and probably should coexist. This is the use of attention-getting audiovisual reports. As far as I know, few foundations outside of the arts and media invite these interesting forms of reporting. But there's little risk in submitting something innovative or unusual, if you remember two guidelines. Don't substitute a media-based report for the more traditional one unless you've been given explicit permission to do so (I'd get that in writing). Second, novelty for the sake of glitz isn't a good idea in the grant-seeking business. The report form should have a rationale you can explain.

I recall when my foundation received our first video

report (as a supplement to a written questionnaire). The grantees clearly had some fun interviewing each other and dragging the camera around to show, in an amateur but competent way, how they spent our money. No fools these grantees – they just happened to include enough copies of the DVD for each of our board members. One picture might be worth a thousand words, but I think it's worth a lot more than a thousand dollars.

CHAPTER 13

Myth Five

It's Fine to Embellish – Everybody Does It

I want to say at the start of this chapter that grant seekers and funders share responsibility for the variously fictional nature of some proposals. Also, in my experience the vast majority of prospective and actual grantees are honest and upstanding people. What I want to pick on here are less the people than the proposals that constitute the lingua franca of foundation funding, especially those involving new or innovative work.

One day, when I was working for a nonprofit, I sat at my desk, cold keyboard in front of me, trying to get going on a funding proposal for a new project. A board member happened by and, seeing me staring into space, asked what the trouble was. When I said I was struggling with a grant proposal, he replied, "Oh, just figure out something we're doing, or something you can say we might be doing, or could conceivably be doing."

He wasn't inviting me to commit fraud; I knew that. Rather, he understood that nonprofits, especially smaller ones, have considerable trouble raising money for unproven programs. He was suggesting I apply for something that didn't exist, without quite disclosing that fact to potential funders. As I used to say in my grant-seeking days, "If we had some ham, we could have ham and eggs – if we had some eggs."

This problem of needing to have money in order to raise money leads grant writers to inflate if not invent program activities. Funders seem to say, "Show me what you've done, be concrete, and list concrete results." At the same time they encourage grant seekers to be innovative, not to get stuck in a rut. Some funders and especially foundation board members are heard to say, "I'm tired of this same old program. How about something fresh?" This seeming whipsaw encourages grant seekers to write proposals that are vague or exaggerated or both.

Funders don't like reading these semi-fictional masterpieces. We don't like seeing decent people pressing against the edge of the truth like blues musicians bending a note. In the end, the problem of credibility is part of what drives funders to support the larger, safer organizations, which over time have acquired the capital to write proposals accurately describing work already under way. Thus the small, scrappy players who might be the real innovators get squeezed out.

Although I'm sure some untruths did occasionally

slip past me, most overstatements and embellishments are easy to spot when you know what to look for: verbose problem statements followed by scanty descriptions of what'll be done, forests of adjectives with comparatively few verbs, lengthy paragraphs full of vague and imprecise language, tangled nests of buzzwords, taking credit for work done by others, and an insistence that the true essence of the project cannot be measured.

My advice to grant seekers is don't lie, don't stretch the truth, don't exaggerate, don't say anything, if what you have to say is so thin a person could read a magazine through it. I'm not accusing proposal writers of being flimflammers; I'm acknowledging that many with payrolls to meet grow desperate and in the cold light of morning would be embarrassed at some of what they've submitted.

If you don't want to end up looking untrustworthy, consider these admonitions. First, don't perch on the slippery slope of honesty, feet extended, ready to push off. Almost every day I received questionable fundraising appeals from decent nonprofits: phony surveys, mass-produced envelopes designed to look urgent, calls from executive directors who said they were in the neighborhood and would like to drop by, and individuals who wanted to discuss issues and obtain my views and opinions, when in fact they were fundraising and my views were irrelevant. These are the small lies of hard-pressed, honest people trying to raise money for a good cause.

A second suggestion is to break down your work into

pieces and sell each part differently. For example, you might separate work that provides *direct service* to affected individuals from a proposed effort that emphasizes *policy change* in that same area, since the strategies would be different and different funders will be attracted accordingly. This piece-by-piece approach is more work, but it lessens the temptation to explain something real and successful, then tack on something you aren't yet doing, making it all look like a single going concern. This misconceived strategy is based on a hope the potential funder won't notice that one piece is real and another isn't. But most funders *will* notice and quite possibly worry that all the work is too fictional or speculative or even nonexistent. No grant is likely to result from a funder who questions the honesty of your proposal.

A better technique is to promote a new piece of work just for what it is, something experimental that isn't yet up and running. In making the case for that new work, you can cite your track record, your successes, your ongoing and already-funded work – but not claim that money granted to your proposal will support more than it really will. To a funder who wants the security of giving money to those who can show they resist the temptation to bend the truth, it's not a minor point. Quite a few grant seekers, especially those pursuing repeat funding, come to the funder with a request for renewal of the grant plus additional funding for something new.

If your organization has been receiving $100,000 a year for your core work, you can approach the funder with a $120,000 proposal to renew your grant *and* add development of a new program that enhances the work already supported. This is like doing the required maintenance of your car and also deciding to balance the tires – you make it all work better.

My third suggestion is that you only take credit for what your organization has really and truly achieved. A distressing trend has been for organizations to take credit for things they did with others who aren't acknowledged. Foundations often make grants to several organizations working on a specific issue. So I was quite likely to have a pretty good idea of who did what in a given field. Claiming credit when it's not your due erodes funder confidence nearly as fast as an embezzlement conviction.

Finally, we need to lay a substantial part of this problem at the feet of funders. I won't take responsibility for your choice to exaggerate or be untruthful. But I know the funding community can make it hard for new small groups to emerge. We place lots of obstacles in the path of innovative or experimental projects. Many funders see their career path as resting on an endless string of undeniably successful grants: foundations end up risk averse.

Writing a perfectly authentic proposal might be difficult, but writing one that's accurate and defendable is something good grant seekers do all the time. When Mark Twain said, "Honesty is the best policy – when there is money in it," he could have easily been talking about foundation proposals.

CHAPTER 14

Myth Six

Funding Is a Cat and Mouse Game, and Guess Who's the Mouse?

Although I enjoyed being a funder, and especially loved meeting imaginative and committed people who worked in nonprofits, there is an unhappy side to most interactions between grant seekers and funders. The granting encounter is characterized by four factors that lead to this dysfunction:

• *Extreme power imbalance.* Funders make the rules, grant seekers must follow them.

• *Lack of reciprocity.* The funder has what the grant seeker wants, whereas the grant seeker ostensibly has less to offer in return.

• *Lack of transparency.* How and why the funder determines the fate of the grant seeker's request may not be revealed completely or at all.

• *Anxiety and fear.* Not infrequently the grant seeker's project, payroll, or organization's future is at stake, but for the foundation employee, it's all in a day's work.

The consequence of these four thorny features of the grantor–grant seeker relationship is a considerable distortion of almost everything transpiring between the two parties. Although most of the people I funded over the years were trustworthy – and I demonstrated my commitment to that opinion by recommending tens of millions of dollars – I know that the fraught, strained, and unbalanced relationship leads to a massive decline in candor on the part of grant seekers, and that funders are responsible for a blossoming of suspiciousness and vast fleets of rules.

Here I want to talk about two features of the relationship that could be better managed by us all: gatekeeping and guidelines.

Let's start with me. The basic problem as I see it is the need for funders to be exposed to the stream of information about new ideas while not letting a trickle turn into a torrent. Grant seekers, as you would expect, want to influence how the gatekeepers of resources see the world and make priorities. The difficulty is, each person sending information to the foundation doesn't realize that scores of others are doing the same thing. What looks to the grant seeker like a reasonable exercise in funder education adds up to a deluge by the time the funder has opened her mail. There were many times when

I tossed a pile of papers into the recycle bin without reviewing them or deleted a column of c-mails, because I felt too pressed with ongoing work to go that extra mile. What gems did I discard? I'll probably never know.

So what about getting through to the funder? In the case of my foundation, the phone is answered by an immensely qualified woman who's charged with this and other duties. She speaks five languages, has a post-graduate degree, has been with the foundation for a number of years, and desires to help people when they call. Yet callers push hard to charge right past her, instead of accepting help from someone who is specifically paid to be helpful.

Other foundations aren't so lucky. When I used to call some of my colleagues, and as a grant maker I wasn't even seeking money, I had a tough time getting through. I felt treated with a lack of respect and frequently concluded that the person answering the phone was little different from the exasperating robo-answerers common among the huge conglomerates we must do business with.

Is there a middle ground, or are funders and grant seekers condemned to snarl at each other from behind their communication devices forever? I want to suggest possible terms for a peace treaty in these communication wars. Funders could agree to:

• Make sure people contacting their foundations are treated with courtesy and respect.

• Employ call screeners who are empowered to offer useful information and refer callers knowledgeably.

• Publish material that tells grant seekers what the

foundation actually will fund.

• Publish a directory that specifies who works for the foundation and in what capacity.

• Respond to pertinent inquiries in a timely way.

For their part, grant seekers could agree to:

• Take time to learn what a foundation supports before clogging the system with unsuitable inquiries.

• Be polite to those who answer the phones.

• Not employ deception in describing who they are and why they're calling.

• Take "no" for an answer.

I don't think this list is necessarily exhaustive, but it offers a good start. I worked hard in my funder tenure to adhere to this set of standards, but, alas, I failed many times. The hardest two criteria for me were publishing material about what we'd actually fund and responding to grant seekers in a timely way.

Disclosing guidelines is a prickly problem, because in a properly run foundation, setting these guidelines is the province of the board, not the staff. Fuzziness can arise because the board itself may not be clear, or may not be united, or simply may not wish to state things unequivocally.

As for timeliness, that's a virtue to which we all should aspire. But as a foundation staffer, I sometimes forgot to do things I'd promised, such as returning a call or giving feedback on a proposal. It's worth mentioning this problem – everyone forgets things on occasion, after all – because it's another instance of the power imbalance. If grant seekers are late on agreed-to items, there can be serious consequences for them. If the funder forgets, it might be that he'd never even notice, and certainly wouldn't suffer negative consequences from applicants.

But let me return to the more serious issue of guidelines. Many years ago, my boss and mentor, the late Herman Warsh, wrote a song gently mocking me. It was called "Just Follow the Guidelines." In the song, Herman humorously pointed out that, although a person like me seems to be forever telling grant seekers to follow the guidelines, he wasn't at all sure that having guidelines was doing anyone any good – either the grant seekers or the funders.

Many years later, I know Herman was right. For a start, I wish funders wouldn't call them *guidelines*. It's one of a number of insincere things foundations do in order to feel that they're not inflicting themselves on grant seekers arbitrarily and unilaterally. Yet when I look at the guidelines my former foundation has on its Web site, I know they aren't guidelines. They're *rules*.

If you write a check, drive a car, vote, or walk around a shopping mall, you follow rules. Why should the rules that foundations employ be obscured by the misleading term *guidelines?*

Funders should be the same as other rule imposers. We should tell you the constraints and limitations in plain language. And then enforce the rules in an even-handed way. Individuals like me sometimes indulge ourselves by pretending things that aren't optional possibly are. We do you a disservice. Softening the message too much might make me feel like less of an ogre, but a good foundation staff person puts aside his own personal needs to do the job well. In particular, I learned to say, "You know, we're not going to fund that," instead of, "Well I'm not sure, send in a proposal." This isn't the same as closing myself off from new ideas. It's recognizing that when I can safely say an idea is outside the boundaries, why waste your time?

And by the same token, enthusiastic and sometimes zealous advocates – that would refer to a slew of grant seekers I've met – not infrequently feel the rules don't apply to them, that in fact they can miss the deadline, or send five pages when three is the max, because their mission is so important, and because they're so persuasive. I used to call this the "I'm special" delusion.

My experience taught me that many who were the quickest to caution me against cronyism and favoritism were just as readily inclined to assume that they were in some way special and didn't have to get the report in, or answer the questions we'd posed as part of our "guidelines."

There are two reasons for funders to publish their rules and for grantees to follow them. One is fairness. If one person stayed up half the night and ran to FedEx to get the proposal in on time, why is it okay for me to say to the next person who's a few days late, oh, that's ok, you needed your beauty sleep, I'll just pop the proposal into the bin along with the ones that arrived on time?

The other issue reflects one of my personal beliefs, albeit one based on some years of experience. I believe that those who are careful and competent in their fundraising work habits are that way in most areas of their work across the board.

So the individuals who get their proposals in on time and include all the required elements are also the ones who show up on time for the city council hearing, who make complete and functional campaign plans, and overall get the job done. I've come to associate those who do a good job of winning grants with those who do a good job – period. This paradigm isn't infallible, but the correlation and impression are pretty strong.

This is a chapter about cats and mice, and I live in a house that has both, on occasion. My cats will always win when they take advantage of their built-in assets of greater power, and some mice meet untimely ends. But I've seen mice endure and even thrive when they've avoided the feline advantage, and played to their own strengths of stealth and cunning. I've met many grant seekers over the years who did the same – they defined their funding campaign not exclusively in terms of funders with superior power, but rather through the skillful use of their own assets and advantages.

CHAPTER 15

Myth Seven

Funders Don't Care

Perhaps the broadest criticism grant seekers lodge at foundation staff is that they simply don't care – about the grant seeker, the organization, or even the issue being addressed. And in an obvious sense this is true.

No one cares about your proposal as much as you, just as a waiter doesn't care the same as you about your dinner. You can apply this thinking to lawyers, hairdressers, most everyone. But the accusation that funders don't care has an underlying element of truth to it, linked as it is to the undeniable impression that many in the funding business are cynical, ill-informed, and lazy.

I was once invited to participate in a private conference that brought together people from a wide assortment of experiences and disciplines to think about an important social problem. We were asked to stay for the entire meeting – several days – so that the small-group process would be effective.

My assigned group argued and strategized and revised our notes, all day every day and into the evening. In the middle of the third day of this marathon, we went out onto the lawn of the college that was hosting our conference to enjoy a warm spring day. As we sat in a circle, intent on our debate, a foundation colleague of mine, who had funded part of the conference, walked up. I knew he was registered because after three days, his orphaned nametag was still uncollected at the registration table. Before long, the latecomer raised his hand and launched into a speech. His tactless natter was irrelevant and inappropriate. After five minutes, while the rest of us carefully studied grass blades at our feet, my friend paused, looked at his watch and said, "Oh, my, just look at the time! I need to go. I've something important to do." And with a satisfied smile at his contribution to our process, he walked off into the sunshine.

We could trade stories, couldn't we, about the insensitive behavior of funders, just as funders have their folklore about the sneaky antics of grant seekers. But there's nothing to be gained from a contest to see which group behaves worse. And besides, in a bad behavior contest, as with many other things, the funders would win. What's worth talking about is what to do with these stereotypes.

I think one root of the problem with the myth that funders don't care is structural. Because of laws as well as traditions, most foundations share certain configurations. Each has a governing board, and in virtually every instance the board works from a founding document or donor's statement, articles of incorporation, and bylaws. Those foundations with enough money and the inclination may hire staff to carry out their interpretation of the basic documents. Because of this common design, we should look at what foundation board members often have as their mandate as well as what various staff are assigned to do.

Foundation boards are composed mostly of people who do care – foremost about the foundation. They're legally liable for its official decisions, which, aside from good stewardship, center on implementing the foundation's mission. The board needs to be sure that the foundation's philanthropic purpose is being well expressed via the grants made in its name.

Does this mean that foundation board members don't care about the grantees? Hardly. I've seen board members tear up for "their" grantees. But in most foundations – especially larger ones – the board is mission driven, not grantee centered. To the extent grantees are able to penetrate the thick wall protecting most funder boards, they may perceive – accurately – that they're not the top priority. But, again, that's as it should be.

As for the grant-making staff, they're usually divided into executive staff (executive directors or in some foundations, presidents), and program officers. Their roles are different.

A successful executive director pays attention to the board's exegesis of the foundation's mission. It is his or her job to make that mission manifest in the world via a coherent and effective granting program. It's also frequently the job of the executive director to help the board determine how best to interpret the foundation's mission in the light of granting opportunities.

Additionally, the executive director needs to work with the other staff – if the foundation is large enough to have other staff – to create a grant-making program that best fulfills the foundation's goals by taking greatest advantage of that particular staff's knowledge and talents.

If board members care most about the foundation, and executive staff care a great deal about the foundation's smooth functioning and mission fulfillment, what do program officers care most about? Is it you, the grant seeker?

Program officers are a disparate group, ranging from flinty Ford Foundation PhDs to young liberal arts graduates from petite family funds. Yet most program staff share an authentic passion for "their" issues and grantees – in that order – and put a great deal of attention into promoting those ideas and organizations within their foundation as well as among their colleagues.

Your grant seeking can be greatly assisted by learning what the particular passions of your program officer are and also where the foundation has been and where it's headed.

With the help of a good program officer and a few

colleagues who have already received grants, you can figure out how to cast your request to hit the sweet spot on the foundation's grant-making curve. Every funder has one. You shouldn't propose a project that represents issues the foundation is just about done with; you also don't want to be so far ahead of the funder that awarding you a grant will exceed the foundation's risk tolerance. Instead, you want to show the foundation's staff that your proposed project will fit perfectly on where they are in their funding curve.

Your second task is getting the lowdown on your program officer. You go around him at your peril; no one will lock you out faster than a program officer who discovers you're trying an end run via another staff person or your cousin's friend's dentist who knows one of the board members. By whatever mysterious process, you've been assigned to that staff person, and you're stuck with him.

What do you need to glean? Mostly it's getting a handle on how much the program officer knows about your issue. Is she a beginner who will appreciate basic orientation to the issues and strategies you know all about, or does she already have a solid basis for encountering your proposal?

If you find you have a newbie on your hands, offer to provide general background material. If it's an expert you're dealing with (foundation sometimes hire experts to run a grant-making segment), do everything you can to find out about her past. Read everything she's written.

This is not as difficult as it may sound, because foundation hires often skew toward academia, a profession that encourages publication. What you're looking for are areas of agreement as well as possible disagreement.

No, I'm not suggesting you depart from the truth of what you're doing – far from it. But you can choose which of your projects to bring to a foundation and anticipate how you'll handle controversial questions before they're asked. The core task for you is uncovering what the program officer cares about and how those interests overlap yours. If there's no overlap, you're in the wrong place.

The single-minded focus of foundations on their own missions raises the question of how they can ever change or learn new things. But truthfully this isn't your concern. Your success in getting funded will depend on your willingness to cast aside any anger or disappointment you feel about "wrongheaded" priorities – or walk away.

Many years ago, when I was working to end the war in Southeast Asia, I visited a dentist who was reputed to be the best and most affordable in my area. This fellow would fill my mouth with instruments and gurgling tubes, and then embark on a rant about nuking Hanoi and his views that Asian people didn't really value life and death the way we white Christians did. After enduring the pain of his tirades – and expectorating – I took my business to a higher-priced dentist who withheld his political views. I suggest you do the same with ill-fitting foundations.

PART THREE

THE GRANT SEEKER'S REALITY CHECK

In my thirty-five years as a funder, I was asked about grant seeking many times. Some issues came up repeatedly, because they were on many people's minds and applied to many foundations. I've made clusters of these topics in the following pages, along with what I think is the best advice for handling each concern.

CHAPTER 16

Six Things You Can Do To Help Your Proposal Make the First Cut

1. Write a compelling summary.

What if you knew that huge sums of money, perhaps a month or two of your organization's payroll, were riding on two hundred or four hundred words? Wouldn't you pay scrupulous attention to those passages? Your proposal will only get read if the summary provides a reason for the program officer to dig deeper. Fuss over the summary until it sparkles.

2. List concrete, specific outcomes of your work.

People want to know what they're getting for their money. That's why so many of the things we buy come in transparent packaging. Your proposal should be a clear container that shows exactly what will result from the funder's investment. Concrete, measurable results provide core reasons for funders to support you.

3. *Connect each step of your work with your goals.*

Many proposals fail to show how specific actions will lead directly to meeting goals. This is a major weakness. Strong proposals are like railroad bridges – steel girders connect every point. Proposal writers too often fail to show a strong connection between their organization's values and its strategies. They think it's obvious. Often it isn't.

4. *Present a budget in standard format that's legible and patently sensible.*

Those who have never used a spreadsheet and those who live and breathe them can be equally injurious to explaining your money plan. By all means, keep spreadsheet jockeys from creating dense forests of tiny numbers. At the same time, don't let someone take his maiden spreadsheet voyage while creating the budget that will be vetted by a foundation's experts. And make sure everything in your proposal is accounted for in your budget. Conversely, omit budget details that aren't fully explained in the proposal narrative.

5. *Get the proposal in early.*

Ostentatiously beating the deadline shows you can plan well and get things done. The reality of foundation deadlines is that if your proposal arrives early, it will stand out, because most proposals arrive at the last moment.

6. *Offer to meet. Once.*

Let the funder know you'd be glad to come by and talk about your work and, if appropriate, bring other staff or board members. If the funder says okay, set up the meeting on her terms. If she's reluctant, let it drop, so you don't provide a reason for her to stop taking your calls.

CHAPTER 17

Eight Red Flags Foundations Are Wary Of

1. *Lobbying or political work.*

Although some funders will support lobbying, most private foundations are wary of work that attempts to influence legislation. If you're engaging in such work, you need a sophisticated understanding of the lobbying rules as well as the ability to articulate why your organization – and your donors – are on safe ground. If the funder appears nervous, it's not a bad idea to show up with a written legal opinion.

2. *High staff turnover.*

Some nonprofits can't provide competitive salaries and fringe benefits and experience their share of musical chairs. Funders know that higher than usual turnover, particularly among top positions, correlates with problems in mission drift and steady funding. If you can show a stable board or consistency in mid-level positions, it'll reassure funders who are considering investing in your group.

3. *Huge gap between top and bottom salaries.*

Some funders will look to see if your top staffers are making large salaries. One measure is the multiplier between the top and bottom people on your pay scale. Is your CEO paid 30 times the amount of an administrative assistant? A way to figure out if your polices are fair – and to justify them to an inquiring funder – is to check the want ads and document that your pay range is comparable to similar positions. Having a written personnel policy that provides an objective series of pay steps tied to employee evaluation can also show that your pay scale is reasonable.

4. *Board composed mostly of famous, and inactive, people.*

There's nothing wrong with having luminaries on your board. What may look suspicious are long lists of "letterhead activists" who lend their names but don't show up. Such a list will raise legitimate questions about who's actually governing your organization. Be prepared to give examples of how famous individuals on your letterhead *are* involved in making decisions.

5. *Board composed of staff.*

Many funders subscribe to the traditional model of a creative tension between volunteer board members and the paid staff who carry out their policies. When paid staff dominates the board, the volunteer dynamic disappears, and not only will funders raise their eyebrows but some state attorneys general may as well.

6. *Extensive, expensive media strategies.*

Let's say you decide the best way to address your organization's issue is to "educate the public." Selecting TV ads or full pages in a metro paper often requires the services of pricey experts and steep placement costs. If you invest a lot of money in something with a seemingly intangible outcome, come into the funder's office with an analysis demonstrating why a media campaign is the best strategy for you. Also be sure to show you have specific plans to measure the media campaign's effectiveness.

7. *First-time filmmakers/writers.*

It is common for funders to receive proposals from those wanting to create a film or book on a problem they're passionate about. Foundations know that absent a track record, these projects are frequently abandoned or drastically changed in mid-course. If you're seeking funding for creative work, it's important to put together a portfolio of past experience and success.

8. *"Hired gun" fundraisers.*

There's nothing wrong with bringing in an outside fundraising expert, especially for specialized projects such as capital or endowment campaigns. Yet this field is famous for problems ranging from inefficiency to criminal activity. Be ready with the details of the outsider's credentials, and prepare specific information on how you'll maintain control of the consultant's activities. Also be able to show how your arrangement with the fundraiser complies with professional ethics codes as well as your state's laws.

CHAPTER 18

Seven Reasonably Easy Things You Can Do to Improve Your Proposal

1. Go on a cliche and gobbledygook hunt.

Funders are as guilty as other groups of lapsing into jargon and affected language. The trouble is, in-vogue terms such as "shifting the paradigm" or "taking down the silos" might not be clear and could in fact mislead the reader. And if the reader has difficulty understanding, he'll be more likely to step out for that second cup of coffee.

2. Use short sentences, active voice, and lots of white space.

Successful proposals follow many of the rules of popular journalism, for the same reasons. They strive to be accessible and even compelling by letting combinations of words create an image in the reader's mind and, in the best of circumstances, mobilizing the reader's thoughts and emotions toward a goal. In your case, the goal is the awarding of a grant, nothing more.

3. *Paint word pictures that draw the reader in.*

Some proposal writers lecture and wag their fingers at the reader. Others become captives of their field's intricacies. Although technical proposals being read by qualified readers can safely use formal language, a proposal writer should pay as much attention to the narrative of her proposal as any short story writer.

4. *Write as much from your heart as from your head.*

Misguided English teachers have ruined too much persuasive prose by requiring a dispassionate, objective-sounding voice. A proposal writer should be close enough to the work and the people who do it to infect the reader with the enthusiasm and dedication of those frontline people. Analysis without feeling is sterile.

5. *Have a good friend edit your prose.*

The harder you work on your proposal, the more difficult it'll be to see the gaps in logic, or redundancies, or passages that aren't clear. To fix these problems you need two things – a good editor and a willingness to accept a critique of your work as help, not a personal attack.

6. *Talk with successful grantees of that foundation.*

Those who work in nonprofits are part of a culture that values helping others, so asking colleagues about their experiences with a funder doesn't have to be seen as helping a competitor, especially when you reciprocate.

Asking colleagues for assistance has the added advantage of building the kinds of alliances and networks that help everyone succeed.

7. When in doubt, don't.

So often, in the rush and stress of completing a funding request, the proposal writer is faced with decisions about what to include. There's a natural but counterproductive tendency to pile on information, perhaps with the thought that bulk is impressive. The end result of these poor editing choices is a mammoth and dense proposal that works against the goal of creating enthusiasm for your work.

CHAPTER 19

Five Mistakes Too Many Applicants Make

1. *Talking mainly about problems, not solutions.*

Grant seekers sometimes confuse writing proposals with authoring pamphlets meant to educate and mobilize the public. Of course your proposal should show you're familiar with the issue, but most of a good proposal will focus on exactly what you're going to do about the problem.

2. *Describing specific problems with general solutions.*

A proposal will succeed to the extent that it provides a clear picture of what will be done about the issue being addressed. Too often proposal writers pour their hearts into the details of the problem and then resort to vague generalities about their actual activities. Offer a concrete action plan.

3. *Prolific use of buzzwords and jargon.*

Some proposal writers confuse density with erudition. What sells the work to funders is clear, simple prose that tells a story or paints a picture. Vague claims, fuzzy or trendy language, and obscure terms don't impress funders – quite the contrary.

4. *Budgets that don't add up.*

It seems so obvious, but enough proposals arrive on the desks of foundation executives with math mistakes to make it worth pointing out how much these careless errors undermine credibility. Not only should the budget add up but it also has to support the logic of the proposal's narrative. Therefore a $100,000 budget to reconstruct sixteen flooded houses won't make sense, nor will $700,000 to hire two new staff.

5. *Parroting the funder's guidelines without linking them to the work.*

It's difficult to understand why so many grant seekers think that pasting phrases from the funder's guidelines into their proposals will unlock the money box. If the funder says they seek to support people working to improve the health of city children, don't tell the funder that your organization exists "to improve the health of city children." All successful proposals need to fit within the foundation's guidelines, but detailing how and why they fit is the key to success, not simply showing that you've read them.

CHAPTER 20

Four Questions You Can Expect to Be Asked about Your Proposal

1. *"What will you do if we only support part of your request?"*

Foundations are wary of all-or-nothing funding strategies, especially when they're pressed by more requests than they can fund. Be ready with a credible fallback position that shows how your work will go forward with partial funding.

2. *"What will you do if you don't reach your funding goal?"*

You won't always reach your fundraising goal. Perhaps the portion you projected from local businesses or from special events won't materialize. Funders want assurances that their investment in your project will be worthwhile even if you have to scale back your plans. Detail concrete, specific, and positive options in your preparation. For example, you can say that you'll cover less territory or take more time if funds come in more slowly than you had hoped.

3. *"Why did you choose these strategies?"*

Some funders look past the overarching goal you're trying to achieve to the strategies and tactics you'll be using. When this question comes up, be ready with a clear accounting of why you chose your strategies, emphasizing their suitability for your particular set of circumstances.

4. *"What will the situation you're addressing look like in three/five/ten years?"*

More than a few boards are encouraging staff to show how their foundation's grant making will play out in the future – for the foundation, for the organization receiving funds, and for the people being served. Foundations are increasingly engaging in the kind of long-range planning they prescribe for their grantees. You aren't being asked to predict the future. Rather, you're being given an opportunity to demonstrate that your current work is solidly connected to real results. You'll also do yourself a favor by emphasizing that your group intends to stay engaged for the long haul.

CHAPTER 21

Don't Be Too Concerned About These Three Peripheral Matters

1. Letters of reference.

Some funders ask for letters of reference, which you should include. But if they aren't required, references rarely mean anything. To my knowledge, there's not a single instance of a proposal that included a letter suggesting that funding be denied. Use references when they add a specific piece of information that needs to come from an outsider. For example, if you're asking for funding to construct post-disaster housing, you could include a letter from a previous project thanking you for getting solid structures up on time and under budget.

2. Fancy binders and colorful papers.

Proposals are read for content. Program officers have already seen every type of decorative paper and binder. In many foundations, proposals are photocopied, which means colored or odd-sized papers end up looking shabby.

Stick with professional, dignified, and simple presentations, unless yours is a graphic arts project where demonstrating your creative prowess is part of the funding request.

3. *Piles of newspaper clippings.*

Sometimes clips are useful. But the mere mention of an organization in a long article doesn't add to the funding decision. Clips should say something specific that connects to your organization's work. And clippings shouldn't be tossed into the package, but rather mounted on plain paper along with a brief explanation of why you've included this information.

CHAPTER 22

Four Things You Should Never Do When Approaching Foundations

1. *Tell the funder to change its guidelines to fit what you do.*

People carried away with the importance of their work sometimes forget to turn off their advocacy. Your job in raising money is to identify a funder whose work fits yours. If you're told there's no fit, look elsewhere.

2. *Ask the funder to help you write your proposal.*

If a funder raises a question about a particular aspect of your proposal, there's nothing wrong with asking her if expressing it differently or adding something might help. But asking what you should say to start the flow of funding will most likely cause the funder to avoid talking with you, a deadly situation in fundraising.

3. *Ask the funder to recommend other funders.*

The one reference that counts with funders is when

they see who's already given you a grant. If you ask for the names of possible donors before the funder has made a decision to fund you, you're showing that you're at best inexperienced and at worst lazy. There are few funders who will welcome being asked to speculate, do your research for you, or share their address books. Let your list of supporters do the talking.

4. *Ask for an "emergency" grant.*

A very small number of funding sources provide emergency money – and even then, under rather specific conditions. In almost all other instances, declaring your situation an emergency portrays your organization as unstable, a bad bet for an investment.

CHAPTER 23

Five Questions to Ask When Meeting with the Program Officer

1. Are there things I can add to strengthen my proposal?

You can't just come out and say, "How do I get money around here?" It's better to couch your question in terms of your proposal and what steps you can take to make it better. And having asked the program officer what to do, you'd better do it.

2. Do you see things in my proposal that could be left out in a revised version?

This is the flip side of the first question: you're asking as directly as possible how to cast the proposal in a way that will play best in that foundation. And when the funder suggests omitting your most favorite prose, don't argue. The goal isn't literary debate but success in obtaining funds.

3. *Do you think I'm asking for the right amount of money?*

It's difficult to know how much to ask for, though of course a review of the foundation's recent grants will give you a guideline. Don't shoot for the moon, but don't ask for too little either. One time a group that asked us for $100,000 received over $2 million. Just try to state your question as a request for advice, not asking the program officer to do your work for you, which could cause offense.

4. *Is there anything else I can do that would help you in your deliberations?*

This isn't quite the same as the first and second questions, which are focused on revising the proposal. In this instance you're asking if there's additional material the program officer would like to see or share with his board. Sometimes I'd be reviewing a proposal and there would be an area I wasn't quite getting. I might ask for more information, or samples of work, or testimonials from recipients of the program's services.

5. *Can you give me an estimate of the time frame for this proposal?*

This is more than a polite version of "When do I get the money?" You can receive valuable information if you listen carefully. You might learn the program officer is thinking about deferring your proposal or even fast-tracking it. You might hear that currently there's a logjam of funding possibilities, leading to the choice of your receiving less money now or more later on. But be aware that some funders are reluctant to reveal their time tables. Experience has taught that they can be mightily harassed by anxious grant seekers, when in fact the grant-making time table is rarely under complete staff control. If you get a vague response to the timing question, let it drop.

CHAPTER 24

A Short List of Unequivocal Don'ts

1. *Never claim to be unique.*

2. *Don't claim to be a demonstration project unless you're using that phrase in a narrow technical sense and can prove it.* If the National Association of School Soccer Field Care asks their Minneapolis branch to test a new technique and then pays for sharing the resulting report with their 288 members around the country, that's a real demonstration project.

3. *Don't rely on spell-check or the purported ability of spreadsheet programs to add figures.*

4. *Never criticize the competition.*

5. *Avoid jokes and especially sarcasm, slang, and most technical words and terms of art.*

6. *Don't use colored paper – or scented cover letters* (I am not making this up).

CHAPTER 25

Six Ways to Help Assure Repeat Funding

1. Get your reports in on time.

Here's a chance to demonstrate competence, respect, good planning, and success. When you force the funder to chase you to comply with the contract you signed, you're establishing a counter-productive dynamic. Most funders have long memories.

2. Provide all the information that is requested or required.

The funder has a reason for asking you to answer certain questions – usually because she's comparing your success with that of others. You want to shine here, not end up as a blank box on a chart that goes to the foundation's board. Most commonly, financial information is missing or incomplete, depriving the funder of a key ingredient in seeing your achievements. The most common delay comes from grantees waiting for audits or fiscal years to end. Unless the grant contract specifies otherwise, send financial data that covers the entire period of the grant contract and the full amount of the grant – nothing less, nothing more.

3. *Put the funder on your mailing list.*

Without getting into annoying over-communication, make sure the funder doesn't forget who you are and why he made the grant. This kind of contact is especially key in multi-year funding. You don't want the foundation to look at your renewal request and ask, "Who?"

4. *Send a thank you note.*

There's no need to gush or order flowers. Since the funder worked on your behalf, letting her know that you recognize and appreciate her advocacy solidifies the feeling of relationship, which is central to good fundraising. Buying a package of thank you notes while you're waiting to hear about pending grant requests is a good way to keep your morale up.

5. *Show that you did what you said you would do.*

No matter what grant report format you're given, you need to base the content of your report on your proposal – the place where you wrote down exactly what you were planning to do. Having committed yourself to doing various things, you should methodically demonstrate that you did in fact do what you promised – and the foundation paid for.

6. Explain why you didn't do what you said you would do.

We live in an imperfect world: few things turn out exactly as we hope. Don't duck talking about what was unexpected. Point out what happened differently from what you had planned or hoped for, and give specific reasons why this was the case. Don't make excuses; just be matter-of-fact about the various outcomes, both planned for and not.

PART FOUR

ADMINISTERING THE TRUTH-DETECTOR TEST TO AMERICA'S CHARITABLE FOUNDATIONS

During my career as a staffer for grant-making foundations, a number of charges were leveled at me and my colleagues. From my safe perch of retirement, here are my best and most honest answers to what you might want to know.

CHAPTER 26

Honest Answers to Hard-Nosed Questions

1

Countless organizations submit proposals and months later receive polite, vague letters of rejection. It's almost as if foundations won't tell you the real reason your proposal was rejected.

This is *true.* Saying "no" euphemistically is part of most rejection – screeners for film festivals, banks considering loans, nervous teenagers trying for a prom date.

As a funder, I had two reasons for fuzzy prose. The lesser reason is that it's cheaper and faster to send out a form letter. The more compelling one, for me, is that when I tried explaining the "real" reason I frequently found it was a waste of time and an exercise in frustration. People get defensive and argumentative – and the conversation drags on.

Here's a compromise tactic my staff used. We first sent out the much-mocked form letters – which, by the way, many foundations continually tweak to convey a tone of respect, regret, and finality. Then, if someone we rejected called, I asked my staff to follow this three-part formula:

A) Empathy

B) Information

C) Termination

Empathy in this case refers to a brief, non-patronizing statement about feelings. Not "I know how you feel," but more along the lines of "I'm sorry this didn't work out; it must be disappointing." We start by acknowledging the passions involved.

Next, the foundation staffer provides a reason for the rejection. This is the hardest part to do well, since the reason sometimes is we thought the strategy was dumb, or we didn't think your organization had the competence, or some other harsh judgment. So like parents at a fourth-grade production of *Macbeth*, we struggle to find something to say that rings true but doesn't devastate.

Finally, termination is the key. Having tried to show some feelings and to provide a reason for the rejection, we thank the person for calling and hang up the phone. Knowing the caller may have paid good money at a grant-writing workshop for the (counterproductive) advice to keep the funder on the phone at all costs, this task can be a struggle. But failure to keep it short is how the conversation can quickly degenerate into recrimination and worse – to everyone's detriment.

2

If in either your proposal or grant report, you discuss your organization's vulnerabilities and detail the challenges you face, your words will inevitably be used against you.

Absolutely. If a teen says to his date's parents, "I tend to drive fast and put my hand on your daughter's knee," or if a prospective employee says, "I steal from the supply closet whenever we run out of Scotch tape at home," where will that lead?

The key is to show that your organization is solidly grounded and learns from past missteps. There's a fine line between being honest and using suspicion-arousing words. If you conceal something that went awry and the funder finds out, you can kiss that grant – and possibly your reputation with funders – good-bye. So be honest but also sensible and realistic.

The basic pattern to follow is this: in the proposal you tell the prospective funder what you're planning to do, why, how, and what resources you'll bring to bear. Then, when you report results, account for each of these elements. If you have triumphs to trumpet, by all means brag a little.

By following the usual grant-seeking ritual of inquiry, proposal, grant, and report, you'll be less tempted to frame your report in terms of failures and more in terms of which results were expected and which weren't. Your proposal for establishing a community gardening program might say, "We're going to start two garden plots in our area, recruit at least fifty people to join our group, make twelve weekly deliveries of flowers and vegetables to the nearby nursing home, and grow two hundred pounds of potatoes and twenty bushels of sweet corn."

That winter, when your report is due, it should parallel your proposal. It's an especially good idea to highlight how some items turned out differently from what was expected, and why. You might say, "The last-minute donation of the vacant lot at the corner of 128th Street and Vine gave us three plots instead of the planned two. Although we were able to grow more vegetables and flowers, in retrospect our volunteers were stretched too thin." You might point out that good growing conditions allowed you to make fifteen (rather than twelve) deliveries. That's great news. But don't undermine your credibility by saying you never got around to weighing your potatoes so you don't know whether you met your goal. Instead, admit that it was unrealistic to predict the exact weight of the produce because community members, many of whom had never grown their own food, were so excited by their crops that they simply took the food home to cook. In retrospect, you didn't accurately anticipate this outcome.

3

The chance of a local nonprofit securing funding from a major foundation is slim to none.

True, and a good thing this is. In the ecology of grant seekers and grant makers, appropriateness of scale matters. This is why house cats don't run down wildebeests on the Serengeti – lions do that job; house cats chase mice.

I don't see much downside to the question of scale. Local funders know their communities, the players, the problems, and the strategies that work in their areas – they're the ones best equipped to help local groups. Even so, national foundations I worked for regularly received inquiries and proposals from locally focused nonprofits. Such mismatches waste resources.

These local groups would often claim their work was potentially national in scope because someone could replicate it (they planned to write a report and post it on the Web, after all). But just as the photos I snapped in Melbourne don't make me Australian, a posted report doesn't make the project national or global. A national strategy is just that – a *strategy* for creating change that occurs at a scale and scope you can explain in detail. In thirty-five years as a funder, I never once saw the claim of being a model work out. Everyone is a model for the rest of the world, just as my kids are model children.

4

With the mountain of proposals foundations receive, if the summary doesn't immediately capture attention, your proposal is doomed.

True. If you're in a bookstore, do you buy a book without looking at the blurb on the back? If you're on Amazon, don't you usually scan the reviews? It's not realistic to think that foundation staff diligently read every word of every submission. So although obsessiveness is usually a hindrance in life, it may not be possible to over-fixate about the quality of your summary. That's what dictates whether your proposal itself will be read or not.

5

Society would be better served if foundations spent the bulk of their assets on current challenges and let future philanthropy take care of what comes down the pike.

This question is a perennial on foundation boards. In fact, during my decades of work I've never known a foundation that *didn't* try to address the tension between current needs and the future. So I'd say this one is *true,* even if actual decisions about assets vary with individual foundations.

Having been around the maypole so many times with this issue, I'm less interested in the outcome for a given foundation and more in who gets to answer it. Overall, grant makers – who feel the press of stewardship obligations – tend to take the longer view, whereas grant seekers understandably are sweating out their current budgets.

The U.S. government weighed in on this question in the Tax Reform Act of 1969, which mandates that foundations preserve their endowments by being prudent; it requires a 5 percent minimum payout every year, even if return on investment is less.

Although the 1969 Act was a good start, I wish the actual payout was indexed to an indicator such as the S&P 500. That way if foundations have a banner year on their investments, grant seekers can share in the bounty.

6

The commonly held view that foundation giving mostly helps the poor, and augments our government's spending for social needs, is considerably wide of the mark. Elite institutions get most of the money.

How sad, this is *truer* than it should be. People tend to give money within their comfort zones, and that's evidently defined by some foundation gatekeepers as awarding grants to people who resemble them – physically and in terms of factors such as social class and culture.

Gatekeepers can benefit from hearing from others, especially fellow board members, whose passion is informed by life experience. I recall a first-rate presentation on prisoner issues made to a foundation board. Their experience with law enforcement didn't extend past a polite ticket for their speeding BMWs, and they couldn't identify with rats on their beds or how it feels to be a black man slammed against *his* Beemer's hood by white officers. The proposed granting program never materialized. If there had been one or two board members with firsthand experience of the criminal justice system, they could have helped the foundation's board reach a more balanced, open-minded conclusion.

The Council on Foundations has provided leadership to challenge the homogeneity of gender, race, class, and sexual orientation among foundation staff. We need another effort in the twenty-first century to bring foundation gatekeepers – staff and board – along to a new level that better echoes their public.

7

It seems that foundations face little regulatory oversight. As long as they pay out their 5 percent they're free to do pretty much what they want, even if it means ignoring the actual needs of nonprofits and isolating themselves from the organizations that depend on them.

For many foundations, this is *true* – a real shame. The financial debacle of the last several years has shown that we need better public surveillance of those who insist on a screen of privacy when they're handling money that belongs to or affects all of us – from banks to foundations.

I'd sure like to see state attorneys general and secretaries of state do more to stipulate standards of practice in the grant-making profession. State officials around the United States, using laws already on the books, have begun to threaten prosecution of funder abuses, from excessive board compensation to conflicts of interest. And what about a voice for grant seekers? Since the financial clout of grant makers gives them disproportionate power, formal mechanisms to guarantee the public a voice in philanthropy would help everyone – including grantors – do a better job.

A pipe dream of mine is to require a foundation to invite the board chairs of its largest and smallest grantees to serve on its board. If this were done, everyone would win. The board would make its decisions based partly on the input of people who have the perspective of nonprofit life, with all its struggles and pressures. Additionally, grantees would learn that good grant making isn't simply a beauty contest.

8

Most foundations recognize the imbalance of power between themselves and their grantees, but few take real steps to mitigate it.

This one is *false,* because many foundations do try, earnestly. But I will say I'm a lot less certain how many succeed. In my opinion, every person who works for a foundation should have prior nonprofit experience as a minimum requirement for the job. Boards on the other hand are more difficult to mandate, since many foundations have fixed qualifications, such as being a member of a family or other category.

I think the power imbalance between grant makers and grant seekers is intrinsic in the structure and in the transaction. If that's the case, one way to address it is to develop a code of conduct, not just ringing phrases from professional associations but actual requirements enforced by third parties, just as professional standards are codified and enforced in some professions by state agencies or boards of review.

For example, there are codes of conduct that address the ethical behavior of police, lawyers, accountants, and doctors. Although these codes may be honored only in the breach, they do provide a precedent for illuminating behavior that's forbidden.

Now, before someone yells, "Too much government regulation," I'm talking about states issuing standards for those who are essentially acting for the public benefit with publically supported funding. Should we turn over an important segment of our society to private individuals who can do as they please? Well – we have!

And I don't see why ethical conduct enforcement can't run both ways. To be sure, grant seekers have trouble dealing with high-handed program officers, but funders have little recourse, too, when faced with serial liars and scammers from the grant-seeking community.

9

Foundations are picky about what they allow grantees to charge for overhead, yet many of these same foundations, in what seems an indefensible practice, count their administrative costs as "charity" and include it in their annual 5 percent pay out.

Entirely *true*. There's no reason the IRS can't mandate an overhead percentage for all flavors of nonprofits, including those giving money and those seeking it. It just needs to be done well.

Some years ago the IRS experimented with mandating an overhead percentage. Put simply, the IRS limited foundation overhead spending to 15 percent (later raised slightly) of assets. At the time I thought it went well and was sorry when it was dropped. All the bellyaching from a few foundations made me suspect the IRS was on to something.

But the rule was written without enough subtlety. Pass-through foundations, those that spend all the money they take in each year from their donor or groups of donors in exchange for especially advantageous tax breaks, were put in a terrible position, and not nearly enough attention was paid to defining overhead, to avoid the instant creation of loopholes you could drive an Escalade through. But instead of fixing the rule, the IRS phased it out.

10

Rather than helping nonprofits cover their operating costs, grant makers overwhelmingly prefer to make grants that support specific projects or direct delivery of services.

I regret to inform you – this is *true*. There are two closely related reasons why. First, foundations are – appropriately – under a lot of pressure from the IRS and state officials to be accountable and from their boards of directors to show results. Often, these requirements mean foundations want results that are quantifiable, measurable. Those ideas are frequently reduced to units of population served or some other project-oriented metric.

The second reason is that some foundation boards put their staff under considerable pressure to fund work that board members see as directly helping the community, however these board members might understand the words *help* and *community*. The building of organizational competence and supporting nonprofit infrastructure are some of the goals that can be lost as a result.

Although some grant maker–grant seeker problems are created by both sides of the transaction, the insistence on supporting only projects, rather than "general support," is one I lay at the feet of funders. I don't like to sound too pessimistic, but in this case I can't think of what would motivate grant makers to relent on this habit.

A cynical person – alas, I'm one of them – might claim that funders insist on project support because it keeps grantees on the shortest leash. General support means the money is given for any legal purpose the grantee decides. Letting the grantee choose how to spend the grant moves some of the power from the grant maker to the grant receiver.

11

The purpose of the tax exemption that foundations enjoy is to enable them to meet their charitable goals and to serve the public interest. When a foundation hoards its assets instead, it's compromising its charitable purpose at the expense of taxpayers.

Yes, that's *true.* I have no doubt that foundation assets should be under greater public control, because everyone pays more taxes to allow those funders tax bargains. This charge is an interesting juxtaposition with the previous one about project support. It shows the stark hypocrisy of some funders – those who demand maximum accountability and control over grant receivers but are outraged over the suggestion that they be held accountable for their own publicly derived endowments.

Although I think political realities make the prospect of increasing the 5 percent minimum payout remote, there could be more incentives to reward foundations that do a better job with their endowments, along the lines of reducing a foundation's current excise tax from 2 percent to 1 percent when it behaves in certain ways the government deems better for society.

You could even eliminate the excise tax entirely for foundations that pay out, say, 7 percent or more. Or you could put together a package of behaviors, such as greater payout and more granting of general support, that would cause the IRS to treat private foundations under some or all of the more favorable rules that govern public charities.

12

Generally speaking, foundations loathe cold calls from grant seekers.

Please listen carefully, as our menu options have changed: this is *true!* Whenever my kids leave the house, I'm unable to resist telling them to drive safely, even though it's a ritualistic mantra of the painfully obvious.

Similarly, I've written articles and given talks admonishing grant seekers to review the rules before applying to any foundation, but I think I've had little effect.

Cold calls have consequences. One is that foundations

hire more people to answer the phones. The salaries and fringe benefits of these functionaries are counted as charitable expenditures that could have been grants. Lazy cold callers not only diminish their chances of getting a grant, they also make it more difficult for everyone else to secure funding.

Second, people like me build elaborate moats. In my time as a funder, I was practically impossible to reach. This is because the majority of the calls that came in for me were an irredeemably total waste of my time.

Does my behavior run the risk of throwing the baby out with the bathwater? Yes – I know I might have missed a call from someone with a fabulous brainstorm. I can only hope those with good ideas read the rules and got to me via the established channels.

If you nevertheless feel a need to pitch an idea to a program officer over the phone, first send an e-mail explaining what you want to talk about and why there's value for both parties to talk. This approach has worked with me, although since the call was preceded by a letter, it's not really cold – more kind of tepid.

13

Ask any grant maker, and he or she will tell you that grant-writing workshops promulgate a number of cockeyed notions.

True. The number one silliness perpetuated by some grant-writing teachers is "Go to the top." Time and again when I ran foundations, grant seekers would poke and prod to get me on the phone. In many cases, I was just about the last person they should have been trying to reach, especially when there was a genuine expert in their field down the hall. Aside from wasting their time and mine, this insistence on starting at the top – often accomplished by a little more pushiness than my sense of decorum allowed – ended up leaving a bad impression. By going up the down staircase, you slow everyone down and risk damaging your reputation with those you'd most like to influence.

Here's a second wrongheaded notion: some people are still teaching aspiring proposal writers to frame everything in terms of "goals and objectives." The truth is, in many cases this rigid framework diminishes effective communication. Tell the story of what you're going to do, why, and what resources you'll mobilize. I've seen the most wonderful, impressive work squeezed and squelched into rigid pseudo-militaristic lingo. To best gauge the right tone for your proposal, look at the funder's Web site. See how they express themselves. Few foundations I know of talk in terms of their goals and objectives.

Here's a third canard, a variant of the advice to go to the top. In this version, a grant seeker is advised to get in touch with the funder and explain why his or her work is important even when the published guidelines don't include that particular area and, sometimes, specifically exclude it. I never saw the wisdom of this, since it trumpets to the funder your reluctance to read the rules or follow them. Foundation staff members don't have the power to change most of the rules, hidden boards of directors do. If you want to become a foundation reform activist, this could be a good thing. Just don't do it as part of your grant-seeking effort.

14

Foundations don't really care about the look of the proposal.

This is true on the surface but underneath I suspect it may be *false* for many of us. For years as a funder, I'd stress the importance of getting the ideas across most effectively and discourage people from fretting over proposal mechanics and esthetics. I think I was sometimes unrealistic. Even though as funders we insist we only care about content, how the proposal looks does matter. Those that aren't organized or that contain typos and misspellings or are dense and hard to read – in a close race, they'll probably suffer.

Although overly produced proposals, like any form of trying too hard, can be self-defeating, someone who takes care to facilitate communication and who lets the reader know there's quiet competence behind the effort will have an edge.

15

Grant seekers have every reason to see most funders as arrogant.

Oh, this is an easy one: *true.* Funders are rightly criticized for being arrogant. Even many funders will allow this is a problem, as long as you're talking about *other* funders.

Lots of power with little accountability is as corrupting as you might think. When I was president of a small national nonprofit, I would talk to pretty much anyone who called. I never knew who might be a recruit, a potential donor, or an important media person. But as a funder, I would tell myself, "Oh, I'm using foundation resources efficiently by *not* taking calls or *not* answering all my e-mail." The problem is, it can be difficult to distinguish between a person who won't talk to you out of zeal for efficiency and one who's just self-important.

I have three things to say to you about "funder arrogance" – a term that many would consider redundant.

First, there's little the grant seeker can do about it. Having experienced funder arrogance from both sides of the desk, I believe the best thing for you to do is keep a laser focus on the purpose of the interaction: getting funded. A thick skin and a willingness to "just walk away" will serve you well. Retaliation might feel good in the moment, but it won't serve you in the long run. Reputation matters.

Second, everything will go better if you approach the grant-seeking transaction with professionalism – projecting dignity, self-respect, and independence. Groveling and flattery project the worst image of you and the organization you represent.

The third I address to my funder colleagues: never hire anyone for any foundation position who hasn't worked for a nonprofit. Although everyone in the foundation world is vulnerable to the siren call of excessive behavior, I noticed over many years that the most abusively self-important funders were those who never had to wonder about a paycheck tied to a pending grant, who never had been treated shabbily by someone's inappropriate wielding of unaccountable power. A history of nonprofit work isn't a cure for funder haughtiness. But it's a starting point for efforts to pull funders back toward humility.

16

What distinguishes a great grant writer from a good grant writer is the artistry of the writing.

Not true. What comes to my mind instantly is: great fundraisers pay consistent attention to detail, joined with communicable passion. The best grant seekers manage to become and remain organized. They use outlines, refer to calendars, and their work invariably has a beginning, middle, and end.

Communicating passion doesn't mean soaring flights of rhetoric, extreme language, or threats that the world as we know it will soon end. Often the passion is quiet. I remember when my youngest son was a toddler, if he was anywhere within reach of his mom, he would place his fingertips gently on her arm, while he was doing something else. He communicated a constant and unbreakable affection with a light and subtle touch. Effective advocates communicate their passion with an unobtrusive single-mindedness. They let the facts speak. They put evident effort into clarity, which lets me know that they believe if I understand, I'll join in.

17

Grant seeking is, plain and simple, a cat and mouse game.

Not true, if *cat and mouse* refers to a combination of stalking and opportunistic shifting of tactics. I think such situations are self-defeating. Cat and mouse creates an oppositional relationship, which decreases the likelihood of a good outcome.

People also get lost in other metaphors, such as *selling,* even sometimes *seduction.* Each is problematic because of the tendency of such metaphors to create inappropriate behavior that diverts the grant seeker from achieving her goal. The metaphor I prefer is *recruitment.* You're doing worthy and important work. You're interested in recruiting my foundation to join with you as a provider of resources toward that effort. This tone keeps the focus on you and your work, it doesn't diminish your dignity or mine, and it doesn't create unnecessary tension, defensiveness, or opposition.

18

Foundation boards rubber-stamp what staff recommend.

False. No matter how much pomp you experienced from the likes of me, I was regulated. Many times I went into a board meeting with confident passion for a piece of work, only to leave with my tail between my legs and no grant. Similarly, there were times when I saw funds flow to work that I believed was okay, while wonderful world-changing efforts languished in the reject pile. Grant seekers need to know that unless they're interacting directly with the person whose money is being given away, the outcome of their funding efforts will never be based entirely on rational decisions. And smart foundation staff will never, ever communicate that a grant is "in the bag" until the check has been cashed – and cleared the provider's bank account.

Plant and Tend Your Garden with Care

For a while I ran a nonprofit that published a monthly magazine, providing me with a great opportunity to play editor. One day I opened my mail to find a hand-written note from one of our largest individual donors. I sure had pushed her buttons. She was so angry at something I'd written in the last issue she swore she'd never give another cent, and she never did.

Luckily for our balance sheet, we had hundreds of individuals donors, a few about as generous as my angry contributor, as well as a cluster of foundation supporters, some contract money, income from the sales of books and magazines, consulting fees, and conference and meeting income. So we weathered that storm – and others like it.

One of the great lessons we can learn from the world of biology is the deep strength of diversity. In the natural world, biological diversity enables ecosystems to survive abrupt changes in weather and the sudden rise of pests and diseases. In the funding world, we can see that funding monoculture equates with precariousness. Organizations often hold out for the big score, the one or two huge grants they hope will solve all their problems and enable them to do the things they've been wishing they could do but could never afford.

Even on the rare occasions when grant seekers do hit the jackpot, they run a real risk of extinction, when there's an abrupt change in a foundation board's conceptual or ideological weather, or a supportive program officer gets a better job offer and their advocate is suddenly gone.

So although this book has been designed to help you achieve greater success, the single most important step for a prospective grant seeker is to pause and reconsider whether this form of fundraising is worth the sometimes monumental effort. If you find it is, then devote an equal amount of time, if not more, to developing other sources and strategies.

Plant your funding garden with a wide variety of annuals and perennials, some that ripen fast, others that bear fruit in future years. True funding diversity will sustain you and your organization for many long and fruitful seasons.

ABOUT THE AUTHOR

Martin Teitel has worked in the world of nonprofits for forty-five years, thirty of them for grant making foundations. He has written five books, dozens of articles and hundreds of postings on philanthropy, the environment, human rights, and politics. Teitel has a PhD in philosophy from the Union Institute, Cincinnati, and a Masters in Social Work from San Diego State University. He is a Field Education Supervisor for the Harvard Divinity School. Teitel has traveled the globe as part of his human rights work and serves on the boards of directors of the Indigenous Peoples Council on Biocolonialism and the Francis Perkins Center. Follow his blog at http://saltmarshmarty.blogspot.com.

ALSO FROM EMERSON & CHURCH

Fund Raising Realities Every Board Member Must Face
David Lansdowne, 112 pp., $24.95, ISBN 1889102326

Nearly 100,000 board members and development officers have used this book to help them raise substantial money – in sluggish and robust economies. Have your board spend just *one* hour with this classic and they'll come to understand virtually everything they need to know about raising big gifts.

Asking Jerold Panas, 112 pp., $24.95, ISBN 1889102350

It ranks right up there with public speaking. Nearly all of us fear it. And yet it's critical to our success. *Asking for money.* This landmark book convincingly shows that nearly everyone, regardless of their persuasive ability, can become an effective fundraiser if they follow Jerold Panas' step-by-step guidelines.

The Ultimate Board Member's Book
Kay Sprinkel Grace, 120 pp., $24.95, ISBN 1889102393

A book for *all* nonprofit boards: those wanting to operate with maximum effectiveness, those needing to clarify exactly what their job is, and, those wanting to ensure that all members are 'on the same page.' It's all here in jargon-free language: how boards work, what the job entails, the time commitment, the role of staff, effective recruiting, de-enlisting board members, and more.

The 11 Questions Every Donor Asks
Harvey McKinnon, 112 pp., $24.95, ISBN 1889102377

A watershed book, *The 11 Questions* prepares you for the tough questions you'll inevitably face from prospective donors. Harvey McKinnon identifies 11 such questions, ranging from "Why me?" to "Will my gift make a difference?" to "Will I have a say over how you use my gift?"

How to Raise $1 Million (or More) in 10 Bite-Sized Steps
Andrea Kihlstedt 104 pp., $24.95, ISBN 1889102415

Raising a million dollars is easier than you think, says Andrea Kihlstedt. It's a matter of simplifying the process. Do that and you

www.emersonandchurch.com

ALSO FROM EMERSON & CHURCH

expel the anxiety. Kihlstedt prescribes 10 bite-sized steps. And with nearly three decades of experience and scores of campaigns to draw from, she has plenty of street cred.

The Fundraising Habits of Supremely Successful Boards
Jerold Panas, 108 pp., $24.95, ISBN 1889102261

Jerold Panas has observed more boards at work than perhaps anyone in America, all the while helping them to surpass their campaign goals of $100,000 to $100 million. Funnel every ounce of that experience and wisdom into a single book and what you end up with is *The Fundraising Habits of Supremely Successful Boards*, the brilliant culmination of what Panas has learned firsthand about boards that excel at the task of resource development.

The Board Member's Easier Than You Think Guide to Nonprofit Finances
Andy Robinson & Nancy Wasserman, 111 pp., $24.95, ISBN 9781889102436

With the possible exception of "How do I avoid fundraising?" a board member's most commonly unasked question is, "What do all these numbers mean, and what am I supposed to do with them?" Financial planning and budgeting combine all of our money taboos with that common math disorder, math phobia. But authors Andy Robinson and Nancy Wasserman help trustees and their staff colleagues confront and address this fear - with wisdom, clarity, humor, and humility.

How to Connect with Donors & Double the Money You Raise
Thomas Wolf, 109 pp., $24.95, ISBN 9781889102429

Most fundraisers today are harvesting low-hanging gifts. But development officers and executive directors who reap the real bounty are doing something many neglect in this era of Facebook. They're engaging their donors in a multitude of ways, large and small, as Thomas Wolf demonstrates in irresistible, real-life stories.

Copies of this and other books from the publisher
are available at discount when purchased in
quantity for boards of directors or staff. Call 508-
359-0019 or visit www.emersonandchurch.com

Emerson
& Church
PUBLISHERS

15 Brook Street • Medfield, MA 02052
Tel. 508-359-0019 • Fax 508-359-2703
www.emersonandchurch.com